Up close and personal

Windy Dryden

PCCS BOOKS
Ross-on-Wye

First published in 2002

PCCS BOOKS LTD
Llangarron
Ross-on-Wye
Herefordshire
HR9 6PT
UK
Tel +44 (0)1989 77 07 07
e-mail enquiries@pccsbks.globalnet.co.uk
www.pccs-books.co.uk

Up close and personal

British Library Cataloguing in Publication Data.
A catalogue record for this book is available from the British Library.

ISBN 1 898059 50 0

Cover design by Denis Postle
Printed by Bookcraft, Midsomer Norton, Somerset, UK

contents

preface

acknowledgements

1   how rational am I?
self-help using Rational Emotive Behaviour Therapy   1

2   the personal therapy experiences of a Rational
Emotive Behaviour therapist   15

3   my idiosyncratic practice of REBT   35

4   hard-earned lessons in counselling   53

5   what I wished I'd learned during counsellor training,
what I'm glad I did and didn't learn and
what I'm sorry that I did   67

6   religion, spirituality and human worth   79

7   when being helped by a therapist is different from
being helped by a friend or loved one   87

8   the name change debate: Ellis's real agenda   95

9   Albert Ellis: man of letters   101

10   the politically incorrect Professor:
Dave Mearns interviews Windy Dryden   109

acknowledgements

Chapter 1 was previously published in E. Spinelli & S. Marshall (eds.), *Embodied Theories*. London: Continuum, 2001.

Chapter 3 was previously published in the *Romanian Journal of Cognitive and Behavioral Psychotherapies*, 2001, *1*(1), 17–30.

Chapter 4 was previously published in W. Dryden (ed.), *Hard-earned lessons from counselling in action*. London: Sage, 1992.

Chapter 5 was previously published in *Counselling Psychology Review*, 1998, *13*(4), 15–22.

Chapter 7 was previously published in S. Greenberg (ed.), *Therapy on the Couch: A Shrinking Future?* London: Camden Press, 1999.

Chapter 8 was previously published in the *Journal of Rational-Emotive & Cognitive-Behavior Therapy*, 1996, *14*(2), 81–4.

The author appreciates the courtesy of republication.

preface

Counselling is a personal endeavour and in this book I present the personal side of Windy Dryden. In the first two chapters I outline my experiences of personal therapy and explore the extent to which I use Rational Emotive Behaviour Therapy in my personal life. In the third chapter, I outline the distinctive features of my work as a practitioner of REBT, an approach to counselling and psychotherapy that I have practised now for 25 years. Chapters 4 and 5 are reflections on what I have learned and struggled to learn over the years while in chapter 6, I reflect on what spirituality and religion mean to me. Chapter 7 is a personal view on why seeking help from a therapist is different from seeking help from a friend.

So far, the chapters have been serious in content. But humour plays a large part in my life and this volume would not be personal without this important ingredient. So chapters 8 and 9 are humorous pieces that have gone down well in the REBT community, but are worthy of a wider audience. Finally, controversy and Windy Dryden are rarely apart for too long and I bring the book to a close by publishing an interview that I did with Professor Dave Mearns that was supposed to be published in a leading counselling journal. However, it did not appear and in my view the editor chickened out of publishing it. I don't know this for sure since neither Dave Mearns nor I received an adequate explanation for its non-publication. I am pleased to have it published here since it does deal with one or two controversial issues.

This is a short book. It is meant to be since I am a short person! But I want you, the reader, to come up close and personal and learn something of Windy Dryden, the person. I hope you enjoy the read.

Windy Dryden

1

how rational am I?

self-help using Rational Emotive Behaviour Therapy

I first received training in Rational Emotive Behaviour Therapy (REBT) in 1977 and have practised it ever since. Before that I was trained in person-centred therapy and had some training in psychodynamic therapy, but neither of these therapeutic approaches resonated with me as much as REBT did, and still does. In this chapter I will consider:

i.   why I resonate personally with REBT theory and practice;

ii. how I implement REBT successfully in my personal and professional life;

iii. in which areas I struggle implementing REBT in my life;

iv. where REBT is not relevant in my life.

Let me stress at the outset that my account (and, if I may venture, that of my colleagues) is bound to be influenced by post-hoc rationalisations, and will therefore provide a more coherent narrative than is likely to be the case in reality. It will also be coloured by what I choose to disclose. On this latter point, my self-disclosure will not be as full as you, the reader, may wish. Since I do not know in advance how my revelations will be used in future, I will disclose as much as I feel comfortable about my professional life and particularly about my personal life.

While this chapter is decidedly not a chapter on the theory and practice of REBT, if you know very little about this approach then what I have to say will not mean that much to you. Consequently, let me first provide a thumbnail sketch of REBT so that you can understand to what extent REBT is for me an embodied theory.

The essence of REBT
Rational emotive behaviour therapy is an approach that is best placed within the cognitive-behavioural tradition of psychotherapy. It is based on a particular view of emotional disturbance which is summed up in a slightly altered version of a famous dictum, the original of which is attributed to Epictetus: people are disturbed not by things, but by their rigid and extreme views of things. In REBT theory, these views are known as irrational beliefs and take the form of demands (e.g. 'I must be loved by significant others'), awfulising beliefs (e.g. 'It would be the end of the world if I were not loved by significant others'), low frustration tolerance (LFT) beliefs (e.g. 'I couldn't bear it if I were not loved by significant others') and depreciation beliefs where you

depreciate yourself (e.g. 'If I am not loved by significant others then this proves that I am unlovable'), depreciation of others (e.g. 'If significant others do not love me then they are no good') or depreciation of the world/life conditions (e.g. 'The world is no good for allowing me not to be loved by significant others').

The basic goal of REBT is to help clients to change these irrational beliefs to a healthier set of rational beliefs which are flexible and non-extreme in nature. These take the form of full preferences (e.g. 'I want to be loved by significant others, but I don't have to be'), anti-awfulising beliefs (e.g. 'It would be bad if I was not loved by significant others, but it wouldn't be the end of the world'), high frustration tolerance (HFT) beliefs (e.g. 'It would be difficult for me to bear not being loved by significant others, but I would be able to bear it and it would be worth bearing') and acceptance beliefs where you accept yourself (e.g. 'If I am not loved by significant others then this would not prove that I am unlovable. It proves that I am a fallible human being who is deprived of the love that I want, but do not need'), accept others (e.g. 'If significant others do not love me then they are fallible human beings who are depriving me of the love that I want, but do not need. They are not bad people') or accepts the world/life conditions (e.g. 'The world is a complex place where good things happen, bad things happen — like me being deprived of the love that I want, but do not need — and neutral things happen. It is not a bad place just because I am not loved by significant others').

REBT is a structured, educational, active-directive approach to therapy where, within the context of a good therapeutic relationship, clients are taught a range of cognitive, imaginal, behavioural and emotive techniques. The purpose of these techniques is to enable them to internalise and integrate rational beliefs into their belief system so that they make a real difference to the way that clients feel, think and act both intrapsychically and interpersonally. In this sense, REBT encourages clients to adopt a self-help philosophy. For more details on the principles and practice of REBT, consult Ellis (1994).

Why I resonate personally with REBT theory and practice
Although I was originally trained in person-centred counselling and psychodynamic therapy, I did not resonate personally with either of these approaches. However, I did resonate with both the major theoretical principles of REBT and its practical ethos. For example, years before I became a counsellor I helped myself overcome my anxiety about the possibility of stammering in public by implementing what was in essence a typical REBT treatment approach. I heard Michael Bentine on the radio talk about how he coped with his stammer by

convincing himself: 'If I stammer, I stammer, too bad.' I took this rational statement and made it more evocative by convincing myself: 'If I stammer, I stammer, fuck it!' Then I rehearsed this belief while using every opportunity to speak up in public without modifying what I said so that I did not avoid words over which I was highly likely to stammer. In doing so, I lost much of the anxiety that I experienced about speaking in public and, as a consequence of this anxiety reduction, I stammered less. I believe this example shows that I naturally resonated with the following:

i. that one can help oneself by actively confronting one's fears (the principle of behavioural change);

ii. that one can influence the way one feels by changing one's beliefs (the principle of cognitive change);

iii. that one can help oneself without being in counselling or psychotherapy (the principle of self-help);

iv. that one can help oneself by changing current factors that maintain one's psychological problems without necessarily exploring the past (the principle of present centredness).

The question is: why do I resonate with these and other REBT principles? The short and uninspiring answer to this question is that REBT suits my temperament and character. These are factors which are largely biologically based, which I am easily drawn to and find natural to actualise. These factors are both intrapsychic and interpersonal in nature. Let me then explore some of the elements of my temperamentally based character and show how these lead me to be particularly suited to using REBT in my personal and professional life.

Activity level
I have always had quite a high activity level. I am easily drawn to areas where I can actively do something to help myself and others and where I can be actively involved in personally meaningful projects like writing professional and self-help material. When I reflect in depth on my experiences of personal therapy which have been largely psychodynamic in nature (and which fall outside of the scope of this chapter), I conclude that one of the main reasons why I found these frustrating and largely unhelpful experiences was that they didn't help me to do something active to help myself. Also, when I am not actively involved in personally meaningful projects, I get restless and

easily bored. Thus, I have made several decisions to stop writing which I have broken because I miss this activity. So I have learned to go with my internal flow and give up making promises I really don't want, in my heart of hearts, to keep.

Self-discipline
Without wanting to blow my own trumpet, I will admit that I have rarely had a problem with self-discipline. Again this is largely due to my (in my view, largely innate) obsessive-compulsive traits. Thus, when I make up my mind to do something, I am very likely to persist until I have done it or until it becomes clear that I will not be able to do it. I almost always keep to deadlines and more often than not, I do things well before the deadline (like writing this chapter). Yes, I learned the value of self-discipline from my parents, but have very little difficulty putting it into practice. In short, it 'goes with' the grain of my temperament. In contrast, I learned the value of eating slowly from my parents, but have great difficulty doing so. This seems to 'go against' my temperamental grain. REBT stresses the need for humans to be self-disciplined and to view this as a lifelong project. I resonate with this view and have no problem with it (unlike the majority of my clients who initially view this with something akin to horror).

Self-reliance
Whenever I have had an emotional problem I have been drawn to help myself to overcome this problem. In the past I have failed to do so only because I lacked the knowledge of what to do to help myself, not because I have sought to be helped by others. I have, of course, sought help from others, but these help-seeking episodes have rarely borne substantial fruit largely because they failed to provide me with a sound and sensible course of psychological action to follow which would help me to overcome these problems. When I discovered REBT in 1977, it was as if I had 'come home' so to speak, so comfortable did I find it as a way of overcoming emotional problems. Yes, being an only child helped by providing me with an environmental context where I could easily express my tendency towards self-help, but I firmly hold that it did not originate this tendency. While many only children are natural self-helpers, many are not.

Cognitive and philosophic orientation
I mentioned above that I have a high activity level. I am also very much at home in the cognitive modality. Little wonder that I resonate with a cognitive-behavioural approach such as REBT. But why do I resonate more with REBT than with other cognitive-behavioural

approaches? One of the reasons is that REBT has a decided philosophic emphasis. Far more than other CBT approaches, REBT outlines a philosophy of healthy living that is both realistic (e.g. it acknowledges that humans have a predisposition towards irrationality as well as towards rationality) and optimistic (i.e. it argues that humans can transcend even tremendous tragedy with their spirit shaken, but not broken). It is the combination of the realistic and optimistic that appeals so much to me and helps explain why I never truly resonated with person-centred philosophy (too idealistic for my realistic side) and psychodynamic philosophy (too pessimistic for my optimistic side). Other CBT approaches are either philosophically indifferent or philosophically poorly developed.

Humour
While others may disagree, I consider that I have always had a good sense of humour and fully agree with Albert Ellis (1987) who has said that psychological disturbance involves taking oneself, others and life *too* seriously. Not that I laugh inappropriately at myself, but I regard aspects of life that others cherish such as status, reputation and social standing as relatively unimportant. Thus, I am generally amused rather than angry when I hear of some rumour or other about myself that from time to time circulates in the counselling/therapy rumour mill. Even when I received a verbal warning at work for using profanity in the classroom (not, I hasten to add, for swearing *at* any of my students), I was amused as well as pissed off when contemplating the ease with which one or two of my students disturbed themselves about my language. Although this episode and its aftermath period had its trials, it also had its funny side as college wrestled with attempting to specify occasions when it is admissible to swear in class (apparently when you drop a heavy object on your foot and the expletive is involuntary). For me REBT is the Heineken of therapies, reaching humorous parts of myself that other therapies cannot reach.

Non-religious, anti-mystical orientation
I am also drawn to REBT because it resonates with my non-religious, anti-mystical side. While a number of REBT therapists have a religious faith, the theory does not encourage a 'faith unfounded on fact' view of the world and takes a decided stance against mystical, transpersonal ideas. The idea of a 'New Age' REBT is as likely as 'kosher bacon'. This suits me as I have never believed in God, reasoning quite early in my life that if there is a deity, why on earth (or heaven!) would he, she or it create Lot's wife a fallible human being

and then turn her into a pillar of stone for showing her fallibility? No, I am an ethical humanist by persuasion and easily resonate with this aspect of REBT.

Lone pioneer

Finally, I am drawn to REBT because it is not popular (certainly not in Britain anyway). I am, I believe, Britain's leading proponent of REBT and have been beavering away to make it more accessible on this island. There is a part of me that resonates to my role as a lone pioneer struggling to make REBT's voice heard in a crowded market-place dominated by humanistic and psychodynamic practitioners. That part of me doesn't want REBT to be too successful. If it were, I would lose my lone pioneer role. While I don't make too much of this dynamic, it does exist in me.

Is there anything within REBT theory which resonates to this idea of the 'lone pioneer'? Yes, but in a way that is different from how this dynamic operates in me. I am referring here to the idea that it is important to pursue ideas which are personally meaningful even if it means incurring wrath and disapproval from others. REBT theory holds that it is self-defeating to believe that it is essential to be approved of by others; doing so will lead one to abandon one's pursuit of enduring meaning in favour of receiving approval which is transitory. I note that Albert Ellis himself pursued the promulgation of REBT in the face of severe criticism and personal abuse from the field in the mid-1950s and beyond. In those days he was a lone pioneer. But he did not waver from presenting his ideas whenever he could, because he did not need the approval of his peers.

Having speculated on why I am so drawn to REBT, let me go on to consider how I apply it in my life.

How I have implemented REBT successfully in my personal and professional life

The proof of the pudding of any therapeutic approach is in its eating. So how successful have I been in applying the principles of REBT to my personal and professional life? I think, in my biased view, that I have done so quite successfully and here are some examples of Dryden-centred REBT in action.

i. I practised the REBT principle of unconditional self-acceptance (Dryden, 1999), after I left my lecturing job at Aston University in 1983 and I failed to get any of the 54 jobs I applied for over a two-year period. 'That must have been very depressing for you', people said when I told them about this period of my life.

'Actually, it wasn't', I replied, 'because I had 54 job rejections and no self-rejections.'

ii. I implemented a high frustration tolerance (HFT) philosophy once I learned that I had high cholesterol by adopting a low-fat, low-cholesterol diet and forgoing many of the high-fat foods that I love. Whenever I am tempted to break this diet, I acknowledge that I am tempted, I recognise that I would like the high-fat food, but show myself that I don't need what I want. Not that I deprive myself of all high-fat foods. I have four squares of chocolate every Friday! I have also exercised five times a week for years now and again implement a similar HFT philosophy in doing so. Most of the time I don't want to get up and exercise, preferring to remain in bed, but I push myself to get up while reminding myself that I can stand the discomfort of getting up and it is worth it to me to do so.

iii. Whenever I am in writing mode (which is fairly often) I resolve to write 500 words a day and very often exceed this figure. What if I'm not in the mood? In such cases, I remind myself that I don't need to be in the mood in order to write and push myself to get going. Most of the time I get in the mood after I have started, and even if I don't get myself in the mood I write anyway. In this way, I live a lifestyle which is rarely affected by procrastination (Dryden, 2000).

These three examples show that I am pretty adept at persisting through adversity as long as there is a point in doing so. As I said before, I believe that I have a temperament which facilitates this process, but I still have to push myself when the going gets tough.

Another good example of how I used REBT in action to cope with adversity concerns my reaction to the following episode. A number of years ago I wrote a self-help book entitled *Overcoming Shame*. As usual I finished this book ahead of schedule and effected a transfer of files from a memory card attached to my trusty Amstrad NC200 to a floppy disk. Unfortunately I wiped the files from the memory card before checking that they had been successfully transferred to the floppy disk and, yes, you've guessed it, the floppy was blank. I had lost the whole book because, as I discovered later, I had used one full stop too many while naming each of the files. Initially I went berserk, started throwing things around and calling myself all the names under the sun. I was furious with the world for inventing fucking stupid things called computers, and with myself for being such a fucking stupid individual. Dear reader, please don't be offended by my language. If you are a counsellor or therapist, hopefully you should not be shocked by profanity, and I'm trying to give you an honest account of my inner dialogue at that time.

Well, you might argue this doesn't seem very rational; throwing things about and cursing the world and yourself for making a mistake — a mistake albeit with serious consequences — but a mistake nonetheless. But let me finish the story. This inner- and outer-directed tirade only lasted for about a minute, for I stopped myself in mid-rant, acknowledged to myself that I was unhealthily angry, accepted myself for adding self-inflicted insult to injury, and reminded myself forcefully that my anger wasn't helping me to solve my practical problem.

After I had calmed myself down, I went on to tackle my self-depreciation. Yes, I reasoned, I had acted stupidly, but no, I was not a stupid individual. I was and remain a fallible human being capable of creativity such as writing a book on overcoming shame, and of a stupid act such as failing to institute simple checks that I 'know' 1 should ideally have done. That's human beings for you, I reminded myself, fallible and capable of fucking-up (I am using the actual words that I used with myself at the time because they did help me).

After accepting myself for my grave error, I then tackled my awfulising belief. Yes, I acknowledged, the consequences of my stupidity were serious: six months of hard slog down the drain or into the ether, or wherever my damned data went. This was very bad, but awful, terrible or the end of the world? Hardly. I would always remember the incident, to be sure, but would I, I wondered, refer to this incident on my deathbed as the worst thing that happened to me, let alone the worst thing that *could* have happened to me? Definitely not, I exclaimed to myself. Yes, it's bad that I lost the book. I value my time, and the thought of devoting a good deal of it with nothing substantial to show at the end is difficult for me to tolerate. But losing the book is hardly awful and I can definitely tolerate it and, furthermore, doing so will help me to make the important decision concerning whether to rewrite the book or to give up on the project. Rehearsing these rational beliefs helped me to feel the constructive emotions of annoyance and disappointment rather than the unconstructive emotions of unhealthy anger and depression that I would have experienced over time if I hadn't identified, challenged and changed my irrational beliefs. These constructive emotions helped me to weigh up the pros and cons of rewriting the book, which I decided to do without complaint after I had concluded that this was what I wanted to do and that to do so was in my long-term interests. The result was the book *Overcoming Shame* (Dryden, 1997) in which I discussed this entire challenging but growthful episode.

The final area in which I have used REBT successfully again concerns self-acceptance. The REBT concept of self-acceptance is a profound one (Dryden, 1999). It encourages people to accept themselves for being fallible, unique organisms. I have already touched on how I used REBT to accept myself as a fallible human being for my angry reaction to losing an entire manuscript. Here I briefly want to focus on self-acceptance for being unique. I have a number of idiosyncratic interests. Earlier in life I might not have pursued some of them because I would have believed that a person of my intelligence and professional standing shouldn't be pursuing such interests (e.g. watching boxing and the soaps on television). Now I see that I am a person of complex diversity; that there is no need for me to attempt to fool myself into thinking that I am other than multidimensional. So, these days, I am more in tune with my 'real' self and hardly inclined at all to pigeon-hole myself.

Areas where I struggle to implement REBT in my life

Are there any areas where I struggle to implement REBT in my life? There most certainly are. Perhaps the area of personal difficulty that I struggle with the most is unhealthy anger. I very easily anger myself when others frustrate me in significant ways, when others get away with acting badly or when they receive advantages that (in my view) they do not deserve. I am well aware that when I make myself unhealthily angry I am holding strong demands about being significantly frustrated and about interpersonal unfairness, but I have great difficulty giving up these demands. I do so in the end, but it involves a great deal of forceful REBT-inspired effort on my part and often the effects only last until the next relevant episode.

Why do I struggle so much with unhealthy anger? Because in my view I have a strong genetic predisposition towards this unconstructive negative emotion. Virtually all the males on my father's side of the family have been quick to anger and this can be traced back over several generations. It's not that I fail to see clearly that unhealthy anger has far more costs than benefits, because I see this most clearly. It's just that on occasion (and sadly these occasions are becoming more frequent, the older I get), I experience a powerful push towards unhealthy anger. I am never violent and I do calm down fairly quickly, partly naturally and partly through using my REBT skills with myself very forcefully. But this doesn't stop me from making myself angry very easily the next time some significant frustration or unfairness impinges upon my personal domain. I usually express my angry feelings verbally, but very occasionally have been known to throw the odd piece of furniture around (but not in the direction of another human)!

Another area in which I struggle to use REBT effectively may seem superficial, but it is important to me. As far back as I can remember, I have bolted down my food, often finishing a dish before the person I am lunching or dining with has half-eaten theirs. I find this habit frustrating because I would like to have a long, lingering meal and I am sure that eating more slowly would have a beneficial effect on my digestion. Again, my felt experience is that I am struggling with a habit with a genetic loading behind it, but whether or not this is the case, it takes a great deal of mindful REBT-inspired effort for me to slow down my eating. Even though I may have done this on one occasion, the very next time I eat, I may well mindlessly wolf down my food again if I am not vigilant.

As I said earlier, I like to be active and I find it fairly easy to be self-disciplined. This is just as well because I do struggle when I have too much work to do. When this happens — and typically it occurs when I come back from holiday and have a great deal of post to deal with both at home and at work — I am vulnerable to stress because I try to deal with the pile of letters *too* quickly. Here, my implicit belief is that I have to be on top of things all the time and I can't stand it if I'm not. If I do not mindfully tell myself that I don't have to be on top of things at all times and that I can stand to work methodically rather than quickly, I will tend to try mindlessly to do several things at once and get myself quite stressed. This need to get things out of the way quickly has also led me on occasion to make impulsive decisions which I have later come to regret.

On thinking carefully about the issues that I struggle with, it seems to me that I find it much easier to tolerate the discomfort that is associated with making an effort and being disciplined than the more acute discomfort associated with not being on top of things and being frustrated.

Where REBT is not relevant in my life

REBT is a therapeutic approach which, like other therapies, has two basic goals: to help overcome disturbance and to promote psychological growth (Mahrer, 1967). In this chapter I have concentrated on showing how I have used REBT (or struggled to use it) to overcome psychological disturbance, although I have also alluded to how I have used it to promote growth in the areas of self-discipline and self-acceptance. However, there are numerous other areas where REBT is not relevant in my life. Thus it has little or no impact on my political leanings and it has no bearing on what I find involving or interesting. For example, I enjoy football and am a season-ticket holder at Arsenal. Does REBT have an influence here? Decidedly not. It would be relevant if I disturbed myself about the grim fact that Manchester United beat us 2–1 at home in the 1999–2000 season. But I didn't, so it doesn't. Unlike psychoanalysis, REBT does not seek to take a position on a range of social, political and cultural issues. Rather, it sticks with what it is good at: offering a perspective on psychological disturbance and a set of procedures to help people overcome their disturbance and move toward psychological health.

In this chapter, I have outlined why I resonate with REBT, how I have used it successfully in helping me to overcome my own disturbance and to further my own development, and I have discussed areas where I struggle to use REBT effectively. In all other areas of my life, REBT has little or no relevance — and that, in my opinion, is as it should be.

References

Dryden, W. (1997) *Overcoming Shame*. London: Sheldon.

Dryden, W. (1999) *How to Accept Yourself*. London: Sheldon.

Dryden, W. (2000) *Overcoming Procrastination*. London: Sheldon.

Ellis, A. (1987) 'The use of rational humorous songs in psychotherapy'. In W. F. Fry, Jr. & W. A. Salameh (eds.), *Handbook of Humor in Psychotherapy: Advances in the Clinical Use of Humor*. Sarasota, FL: Professional Resource Exchange Inc.

Ellis, A. (1994) *Reason and Emotion in Psychotherapy* (revised and expanded edition). New York: Birch Lane Press.

Mahrer, A. R. (ed.) (1967) *The Goals of Psychotherapy*. New York: Appleton Century Crofts.

2

the personal therapy experiences of a Rational Emotive Behaviour therapist

Introduction

In Britain today, most professional bodies require psychotherapists to have had personal therapy before being registered or accredited. While professional bodies representing different therapeutic approaches specify the length and frequency of such personal therapy, this is not the case with more general professional bodies. Both the British Association for Counselling and Psychotherapy and the Division of Counselling Psychology of the British Psychological Society now specify that accredited (in the first case) and chartered (in the second case) practitioners have to have a minimum of 40 hours personal therapy. What is so magical about 40 hours? Neither body has given a convincing argument for this figure and certainly not one that stems from the research literature.

When I began my training as a counsellor in Britain (in 1974), there were few general accrediting professional bodies and very little guidance (outside the analytic tradition) concerning whether to seek personal therapy, let alone what type one should seek and how long and how frequently one should seek it. What follows, then, is an account of my personal therapy experiences from my contemporary position strongly in the Rational Emotive Behaviour Therapy (REBT) tradition.

In recounting my history of personal therapy I will cover experiences of individual and group therapy that I had before my training as a counsellor and after I began training. I will also discuss the personal development groups that I attended which were a mandatory part of three periods of my professional training. Finally, I will discuss instances of self-help because they illuminate why I derived so little help from consulting my fellow practitioners. After relating each episode (or related episodes) of personal therapy, I will comment on my experiences.

Three funerals and a wedding

The first time that I entered personal therapy was at the end of 1974. I had just started my professional training as a counsellor and at the age of 24 years, I was suffering from general feelings of unhappiness, a sense that my life was something of an effort even though I had clear vocational goals and was pursuing them. Had I completed the Beck Depression Inventory at that time, I would have scored in the mild to moderate range of depression. So I decided to seek personal therapy, partly to deal with this state of unhappiness, but also because I thought that I *should* be in personal therapy given that I was training to become a counsellor. Even though there was no edict at that time from any professional body that I was associated with, there was a 'feeling' that being in personal therapy was 'a good thing', a view that was expressed by the various psychoanalytic associations. In Britain, at that time (and to a lesser extent today), counselling in Britain was dominated by psychoanalytic and person-centred practitioners. The person-centred school recommended the inclusion of personal development groups in the therapeutic curriculum and the psychoanalytic school recommended personal therapy as a mandatory activity which had to take place away from the training institution where one was being trained.

I do not recall why I chose to seek a psychoanalytic personal therapist, but I do remember at that time uncritically accepting what I now consider to be a myth that psychoanalytic therapy is 'deeper' than other approaches.

Funeral 1
I am being somewhat unkind to therapists in this account by referring to my experience with them as *funerals*. What I mean to convey is that they were more or less ineffective from the point of view of helping me overcome my malaise. My first therapist was a middle aged, male Jewish therapist (as I am now) and, I think, a Kleinian. My uncertainty stems from the fact that the person who referred me to him only said he was psychoanalytic by persuasion. My therapist certainly didn't tell me anything directly about his therapeutic orientation and I didn't ask because at that time it never occurred to me to ask.

This therapist was not austere in his demeanour, but neutral and strictly interpretative. Whenever I was speaking he buried his head in his hands, and on the infrequent occasions when he was about to say something, he would rock forward, take his hands away from his mouth, make an interpretation — which I largely found puzzling — and then return to his normal pose. My attempts to seek clarification about his interpretations were met by silence or by a further interpretation along the lines that I wanted him to feed me (hence my guess that he was Kleinian). Indeed, as I recall, this was his favourite interpretation.

This therapy was unstructured and open-ended. I had the sense that I could talk about whatever I wanted and that I could see him for as long as I wanted. Actually, the therapy lasted for about six months of weekly sessions because I was moving away from London and was reluctant to make the weekly trips back to London to see him. While I was not sorry to end, I have always wondered how it would have (and indeed if it would have) progressed had I stayed. One thing was clear at the end of this episode of personal therapy: I still experienced the same sense of unhappiness.

Funeral 2

My second venture into personal therapy was with a psychiatrist who taught a module on 'Psychiatry' in the counselling programme that I had finished in July 1975 and in which I made the transition to lecturer in August 1975. I asked this man for a recommendation for someone who might take me on since I still wanted to get to the bottom of my unhappiness. He suggested that he could see me himself in his National Health Service clinic at the local psychiatric hospital. I should add in his defence that the issue of dual relationships was not as sharply drawn as is now the case. I was just pleased at his suggestion and gratefully accepted his offer.

I knew that this second therapist was also psychoanalytically oriented, but he was far more interactive than my previous therapist. He also practised psychodrama, and we used several psychodrama techniques over the time that I saw him. About five or six months after I had started to see him, he told me that he had to end the therapy because he was leaving his practice to work full-time as a Senior Lecturer in Psychiatry. I understood this and experienced a good sense of closure since he also arranged for me to see a colleague in the same clinic. My abiding memories of this second episode of personal therapy was that my therapist took voluminous notes at the beginning which I found off-putting. However, he was quite happy to stop doing so when I asked him to. I also remember the psychodrama techniques and found them quite useful in getting me out of my head and more into my experience. My most vivid memory, as I look back on this experience, was that we both smoked cigars during therapy sessions, but that his were longer than mine!

There was again no therapeutic contract at the beginning and, like my first experience, it had an open-ended quality about it. However, as you may have surmised, my feelings of unhappiness persisted.

Funeral 3

I was then referred to a man who was one of the few fully trained psychoanalysts working in the Midlands. However, he did briefer work in the clinic where I saw the second therapist and, as indicated above, he agreed to take me on at the request of that person. In all, I had eight sessions with this man, an experience which I found quite frustrating. Again there was no therapeutic contract and no agreed time limit as part of this contract. In my innocence, I was operating on the assumption that again the therapy would be open-ended. My third therapist was neutral and cold with it. Looking back, I never experienced my first therapist as cold even though he was strictly neutral. Somehow, I sensed that he did have a concern for my well-being. However, this was not the case with my third therapist. I also remember, on one occasion, asking him whether what I was experiencing was transference and received quite a sarcastic reply. No, this man didn't show any concern for me as I look back and this was also how I felt at the time.

I am drawn to books on therapy which seek to explore key therapy moments, crucial sessions and turning points in the therapeutic process. For I can still remember quite vividly the eighth and final session that I had with this man. He began the session by announcing that this was to be our last session. I am very sure looking back that we had not agreed on an eight-session contract (or any other time-limited contract) and my sense of shock and bewilderment at the time strengthens me in my retrospective view on this point. He then said casually, and this is really clear in my mind, that if I wanted to continue to see him then I could do so in his private practice. I can't recall how I responded to this other than to decline the invitation and to get myself out of his office as soon as I could. The lasting impression that I have of this man is that he was arrogant. I recall him being late for one session and offering no apology or explanation for his behaviour. When I brought this up in the session he dismissed my legitimate complaint and proceeded to interpret my reaction.

I remember to this day feeling dazed as I made my way home after the final session. I just couldn't believe what had happened. Had I imagined it? Had I offended him in some way? I was given no explanation for this abrupt termination except that this was to be the last session.

. . . and a wedding

Having been dismissed by this third psychoanalytic therapist, I decided to fall back on my own resources. Earlier in my life I had overcome my public-speaking anxiety which I developed due to my attitude towards a speech impediment by implementing a technique that I heard described on the radio. In brief, I resolved to speak up at every opportunity — without recourse to the myriad of ways I had developed to prevent me from stammering — while telling myself: 'If I stammer, I stammer. Fuck it!' Not only did I largely overcome my anxiety by this method, I stammered far less than hitherto.

Those of you who know anything about Rational Emotive Behaviour Therapy (REBT) will recognise this as an unschooled version of one of its major techniques: the rehearsal of a rational belief while simultaneously confronting one's fears. Consequently, it will not come as too much of a surprise to learn that in 1976 I turned for inspiration to *A New Guide to Rational Living*, an REBT self-help book written by Albert Ellis and Robert Harper (1975) . We had briefly studied REBT during my counselling programme a year or so earlier, and I remembered resonating to Ellis's ideas about the theory and practice of psychotherapy, but didn't have time to study REBT in depth because we were mainly concerned with the work of Carl Rogers.

On reading about the REBT perspective on psychological problems and their remediation I quickly saw that my unhappiness was due to feelings of inferiority about various personal issues. I further realised that the reason I suffered from such feelings was because I held a number of irrational beliefs about myself in relation to achievement and approval. At last, I had found what I was looking for: an approach which spelled out for me a perspective that I could make sense of and relate to (that I was unhappy because of the rigid and extreme beliefs that I had about myself) and a way of overcoming these feelings (by identifying, challenging and changing these beliefs using a variety of cognitive, imaginal, behavioural and emotive techniques).

So my self-help therapy gave me what my therapist-delivered therapy failed to — clear information about a conceptualisation of my psychological problems that I accepted and specific guidelines of how to overcome these problems. Not one of my three individual therapists gave me any kind of account of how they conceptualised my problems, and none of them gave me any guidelines at all concerning how to remediate these problems. I am not saying that all clients require such clarity, but I certainly did. If they had given me specific directions about conceptualisation and treatment, I could have given my informed consent to proceed or decided that I did not want to continue.

You may be wondering whether I was not given this information because I was expected to know it being a trainee counsellor. I doubt this because (a) openness was not a feature of my therapists' behaviour in other areas and (b) they did not even inquire of me whether I wanted this information. Therefore, if any of my therapists decided not to give me information about conceptualisation and treatment because they thought I would know this already, then they were sadly mistaken.

Comments
None of my three therapists made any significant attempt to explain to me how they conceptualised psychological problems in general or my problems in particular. This is what Bordin (1979) considers a key therapist task and forms an important part of eliciting informed consent from the patient. Thus, none of my three therapists elicited my informed consent to proceed with therapy. While some would regard this as an ethical oversight, I will be charitable and say that my

therapists were following the analytic tradition where such explicit explanations are generally eschewed. Clearly, this lack of explanation did not meet my psychological 'need' for explicitness. I am a person who likes to know clearly what help I am being offered so I can make my own mind up whether or not I wish to proceed. My attempts to elicit such clarity were either ignored, interpreted or, in the case of my third therapist, ridiculed. Why did I not decide earlier that psychoanalytic therapy was not for me? Simply because I did not have the confidence in my judgement to do so.

Looking back, I thought that if I stayed in psychoanalytic therapy long enough, I would be helped by the process, despite evidence to the contrary. This taught me that clients may place too much faith in their therapists who they think know what is best for them. As a therapist, I emphasise to my clients that what I have to offer them is one approach to understanding client problems and how to address them, and I stress that there are other approaches available. I tell them that if what I have to offer is not perceived as helpful to them then they are not to blame and that I will make every effort to refer them to a practitioner who may be able to help them more effectively. As my friend and colleague, Arnold Lazarus (Dryden, 1991) has said, making judicious referrals is a skill and a mark of therapist maturity. None of my individual therapists raised this as a possibility. Did they fail to do so because they knew I was a therapist-in-training and thought that I could be expected to know about their approach to that therapy they were practising? Did they assume that I had already made an informed decision that I wished to proceed with therapy in each case? As I said earlier, I doubt that they had made such assumptions and even if they had, then they were in error. What I have learned from this is not to assume that therapists in training or even trained therapists have given informed consent to proceed without explicitly eliciting such consent first, unless there is powerful evidence to the contrary.

None of these three therapists discussed in this section explained to me what my tasks were in therapy or for that matter explained what tasks they were going to engage in during the therapeutic process. My guess is that either I was expected to know as a counselling trainee, or more likely I was expected to just talk about whatever I was disturbed about at the time. It was all very unstructured and loose when I needed clarity and structure. The exception to this was the second therapist who asked me if I wanted to try out some psychodrama techniques on several issues that I was exploring. My recollection was that this therapist introduced the possibility of using these techniques in a relaxed, non-pressuring way and I was pleased with both the offer and how it was made.

Bordin (1979) has argued that it is important for therapist and client to agree on the latter's *goals* for change. This does not mean that the therapist uncritically accepts the client's goals. Rather, it means discussing openly the issue of goals so that agreed objectives emerge from such dialogue. It would have been helpful to me if my individual therapists had initiated such a discussion (for I do believe that it is the therapist's responsibility to do so). While I now understand the psychoanalytic position on goals, I did not realise this then and therefore I was looking towards my therapists for guidance on this issue — guidance which never came. Even if I couldn't realistically have expected my therapists to change their practice to accommodate to my preference, was it too much to expect them to elicit my position so that they could judge whether I was suitable for their mode of treatment? I think not. Again, in my practice, I attempt to elicit my clients' views on this point and I am clear with them concerning my position on eliciting goals for change.

It should be clear by now that none of my therapists understood what I thought might be most helpful to me from therapy. Such understanding forms one important part of what Bordin (1979) refers to as the *bond* component of the working alliance. Another aspect of the bond relevant to these personal therapies concerns the interpersonal connection between therapist and client. The relationship between the first therapist and myself was fairly neutral. Behind his steadfast interpretative stance, I sensed he was a fairly kindly man, but this was only a shadowy impression.

As I said earlier, I knew the second therapist in a different context in that he taught in my counsellor training programme when I was a student and continued to teach this module during the time that I consulted him when I was lecturing on the same course. So I knew him in other contexts and experienced him as someone who was reasonably caring. This side of him came to the fore after I had requested that he stop taking notes and give me greater face-to-face contact. Before this I sensed that he was hiding behind his psychiatrist role. He responded well to my request and from that point I would characterise our therapeutic relationship as two colleagues, one senior and the other junior, working to help the latter towards some unspecified goal. Of all the individual therapists that I consulted, he was the one who best understood my need to be active in therapy and suggested on occasion that we use psychodrama techniques. I would say that of the three therapists discussed in this section, I had the smoothest relationship with him and the most difficult relationship with the third therapist.

I didn't have the sense that the third therapist was listening attentively to me. He may have been, but as Rogers (1957) wisely said, for the core conditions to have a therapeutic impact on the client, the client has to experience their presence. If the therapist is listening attentively and the client does not experience this then there will accrue no positive impact for the client. Indeed I experienced him as detached, uncaring and somewhat arrogant. The way he abruptly and unilaterally terminated therapy accompanied by the offer that he could continue to see me as a patient in his private practice showed the somewhat exploitative nature of this man's work with me and perhaps his greed. In brief, I didn't much care for him and sensed also that he didn't much care for me. By today's standards, I suppose one could argue that there were abusive elements to this relationship. I am thinking here of his unilateral announcement, without any prior warning, that he was terminating the therapy.

To be charitable, one might argue that in 1976 the importance of planning for termination was not as much appreciated as it is now and the practice of moving patients from the National Health Service where therapy is free to the private (fee-paying) sector may not have been viewed as unethical as it would be now. However, this man was a fully trained psychoanalyst, for goodness sake, and a full member of the Institute of Psychoanalysis, one of the most prestigious psychoanalytic institutes in the world. Even at that time, I am sure that his colleagues would have been shocked by his behaviour towards me. The fact that I used this experience to very good effect should not be used to condone this behaviour.

I described earlier how I gave up on therapist-delivered therapy and turned, with good results, to self-help. Why was this experience more effective for me than over one year's therapy delivered by well qualified practitioners? First, I resonated much more with the REBT explanatory model than with the psychoanalytic one, such as I understood it. I liked the fact that when I read Ellis and Harper's (1975) *A New Guide to Rational Living*, the authors, from the very outset, made perfectly clear how they conceptualised emotional disorders. However, even if my therapists had clearly stated the psychoanalytic view of psychopathology, I would still have favoured the REBT view. Why? Because, it emphasised the role of cognitive factors which struck a real chord with me in helping to understand not only my own problems, but also those of my clients. Up to that time, I was still practising person-centred therapy, but my encounter with this REBT self-help book and my subsequent successful self-help efforts led me to decide to re-train in REBT, a decision I have never regretted.

Second, I resonated with the REBT's direct, clearly understood and, some would say, no-nonsense approach to dealing with one's emotional problems. It was never really clear to me how talking in an open-ended way, as in my psychoanalytic therapies, would help me to overcome my sense of unhappiness, but it was crystal clear to me on reading Ellis & Harper's (1975) book what I needed to do to free myself of these feelings. I needed to identify, challenge, and change my irrational beliefs and act in ways that were consistent with the rational alternatives to these beliefs. Simple, but not easy, as we say in REBT.

For me, one of the problems with these individual therapies was that they were too open-ended with respect to goals. None of my therapists asked me what I wanted to achieve from therapy. When I began to use REBT with myself, I not only asked myself what my problems were, I asked myself where I wanted to be with respect to each of these problems. I saw that my problems at the time were to do with feelings of inferiority and I wanted to be more self-accepting. The REBT position on unconditional self-acceptance (Dryden, 1999a) was a revelation to me. It encouraged me to view myself as equal in humanity to all other humans, to fully acknowledge my weaknesses as well as my strengths and to appreciate that the existence of the former did not mean that I was inferior and that I could address them non-defensively. Carl Rogers' (1957) notion of unconditional positive regard did not have a similar impact on me since it was, as I saw it then, encouraging people to prize rather than to accept themselves.

Having a clear idea of where I was headed on this issue as well as how to work towards getting there were key ingredients to the progress that I made in overcoming my unhappiness. I should add that in my over-enthusiasm I did not appreciate at the time that it is not possible to achieve perfect self-acceptance. I realise now that this is a life-long process and whereas I am far more self-accepting now that I was then, I still have my vulnerabilities in this area. This fact, however, does not discourage me.

It is perhaps strange to think of developing a bond with yourself, but in self-help that is precisely what happens. In helping myself overcoming my malaise, I developed a more accurate understanding of myself than that shown by my personal therapists towards me. This was because I used the REBT perspective to understand myself. Note that I could not use the psychoanalytic perspective to do this, nor was I helped to do so by any of my personal therapists. Finally, an important aspect of the therapeutic bond is pacing. All of my therapists worked too slowly with me, another feature of the psychoanalytic approach with which I did not resonate. By contrast, when I used REBT to help myself, I was able to do so at my own, quicker rate. From all these experiences, I have learned the following which I routinely implement in my practice as a therapist.

i.   I explain to clients exactly what REBT is and outline broadly the kinds of tasks that I am likely to implement and the kinds of tasks they will be called upon to engage in. I elicit their reactions and, if they indicate that REBT is not the type of therapy they are seeking, I refer them to a therapist who is likely to meet their treatment preferences as long as these preferences do not perpetuate the clients' problems.

ii.   I help my clients to specify their problems and what they want to achieve with respect to each of these problems. Then I focus therapy on helping my clients to achieve their goals.

iii.   I strive to develop the kind of bond that will facilitate the treatment process and if I consider that any of my colleagues can better develop a preferred bond with any of the people that are seeking my help, I do not hesitate to effect a suitable referral. I am fortunate that financial considerations do not compromise my position on this issue since I am not dependent upon my practice for my livelihood.

Having described and commented on my experiences of both therapist-delivered and self-help therapy, let me move on to my experiences of being a member of a therapy group which I joined in the final year of my undergraduate degree. This experience therefore occurred before I began to train as a counsellor.

One year of group therapy
Actually, the therapeutic experiences I have just related were not my first experience of being a client. In May 1970, towards the end of my second year of my undergraduate degree, I decided to stop working for my exams and to feign illness. I was sent to see the college psychiatrist who decided that I needed to join a psychodynamic group that was being convened at the beginning of the next academic session in October 1970 that he was running with a psychiatrist colleague. In the interim, however, I finally got my act together and resat the exams in July which I duly passed.
    I dutifully joined the group, which comprised about eight patients and two therapists, who both took a fairly inactive, interpretative role.

I did admit to the group that I had feigned illness after about six months, but since I was well over my crisis by then, this disclosure didn't really help me. Looking back, I think that my stopping working and feigning illness was an attempt to get out of something that I did not enjoy (second-year psychology topics are notoriously tedious) and I hoped that I could go into the final year of the course on the basis of my course work in lieu of passing the exams. Once I had tested the system and realised that I couldn't avoid the second year examinations, I faced up to my responsibilities and studied hard from that point forward. My decision to take responsibility did not come from my participation in the group since all this happened before I joined the group.

I did learn one thing from the group sessions which proved to be a valuable life lesson. I became friendly with one of the group members and we started to meet socially (which, if I recall, was not prohibited by our group membership). This friendship turned out to be very one-sided and if I did not contact him, he wouldn't contact me. Initially, I disturbed myself about this lack of reciprocity and even confronted him about it in the group. He apologised, promised to initiate contact, but didn't. At this point, I remember changing my attitude about it. I reasoned that he was the person he was and not the person I expected him to be and if I wanted to be friends with him, I had to realise that I would have to initiate contact because he wasn't going to. Once I accepted this grim reality, I calmed down and decided to remain friends with the guy. He never did initiate contact, but I was undisturbed about it. Looking back on this episode, it occurs to me that I never shared my self-authored insight with the group since I tend to work things out in my head rather than through dialogue with other people.

So what else did I learn from being in the group? Precious little other than psychodynamically oriented groups were not for me. This was a lesson that I had to relearn several times as I will presently discuss. Of course, some would say that being a member of the group helped me to come to this realisation, and indeed this may be true despite my protestations to the contrary. However, this hypothesis is impossible to disprove. All I can say is that it didn't seem to me either at the time or in retrospect that being in the group had a bearing on my adjustment to my friend's behaviour.

Comments
Looking back, I really don't know why I was referred to this psycho-dynamic group. Certainly, when I saw the psychiatrist for an assessment interview and he made the recommendation that I join the group, he did not give me any kind of rationale for my joining. My impression

is that he needed to get sufficient numbers for the group to be viable and there were no strong contra-indications that would rule me out as a group member. At the time, I was in awe of this psychiatrist (because of his status rather than his personality) and if he thought that I needed to join a group for one year, then he must be right. After all, he was the professional and I was a mere undergraduate. Now, of course, I know different. As a practitioner, I regard giving clients a clear rationale for treatment as paramount and I make sure that they think carefully about my treatment recommendations before accepting them.

One of the features of this group experience was the inactivity of the group therapists. Much of the work was done by the group members who often gave each other fairly inept advice. When the therapists did intervene it was to make interpretations and if these were ignored, as they generally were, they remained silent. From what I could see, very few of the group members derived much benefit from the year of group therapy.

This experience taught me that it was important for a group therapist to encourage interaction between members, and to intervene frequently in the group process. This assists group members to focus on their goals and presents a corrective force when group members give each other bad advice. The way I do this as an REBT group therapist is to highlight any helpful aspects of the proffered advice, and then to focus on the psychological issues that group members often overlook when they advise one another (Dryden, 1999b). In this way, I strive to reserve the motivation of the group members to be helpful to one another, while focusing the members' attention to what they need to do psychologically to achieve their goals. As an REBT group therapist, I see myself as having a gate-keeping role, whereby I encourage fruitful interaction between group members; and an educative role, whereby I encourage members to use REBT techniques to help themselves and one another. The two group therapists running the group that I have just described were rather poor gate-keepers, often allowing unhelpful interactions between group members to develop unchecked and were poor educators in that they did not provide explanations for their interpretations.

Four tedious years of personal development groups
In all, I experienced four years of being in three personal development groups. Frankly, I found them something of a waste of time. Since they were composed of students who saw one another in other contexts (academic, supervisory and social), most of us were on our guard concerning what we said in the group about our lives and about

our feelings towards one another. Not that such groups were unhelpful for everyone. From what I could see they especially helped socially inhibited members who learned that they could talk about themselves and even confront other group members and that nothing terrible resulted from such disclosures and confrontations. Since I already knew this, I decided to knuckle down and play the game which seemed to be that one talked about oneself at length every five or six weeks and said something in every other group when others were talking. It seemed that unless you did this, you became the focus of the other group members who wanted to know why you were silent or distancing yourself from the group.

I make no apologies for sounding cynical about these groups, but I do apologise to my past students for making them a mandatory part of counselling programmes that I have run. I did so not because I thought that they were of any value but because professional accrediting bodies expect them to be a part of the training curriculum and I didn't want to disadvantage my students by depriving them of this 'mandatory' experience.

Comments
These personal development groups were strictly speaking not therapy groups, but more like sensitivity groups. Group members were not seen as having personal problems for which they needed help, but developing professionals who needed to become more aware of themselves and their impact on other people. This is quite a reasonable activity for counsellors in training to be engaged in, and I wouldn't have objected to attending one such group for a year. What I objected to was having to attend three such groups over a four-year period. My requests for exemption fell on deaf years for a reason that I can understand being a counsellor trainer myself, but which ultimately cannot be justified, since the raison d'être of a personal development group (PDG) is the 'personal development' of its individual members. It was thought that if trainees could exempt themselves from being a member of a personal development group, then this would produce a schism in the training cohort which would split into 'attenders' and 'non-attenders'. Trainers are very wary of permitting any practices which divide a training cohort and also deprive group members of a forum where they could discuss their feelings about the course and about other course members in a group facilitated by a person external to the course. However, I am not speaking against having a forum for course members to discuss the course, although in my view this needs to be done with the course director present.

It seemed, therefore, that my continuing membership in these personal development groups had more to do with promoting harmony (or at least minimising conflict) in a cohort of trainees than with facilitating the personal development of individual trainees. My argument at the time was that my own particular personal development could have been better promoted outside the group setting, and I still hold to this view.

I mentioned earlier in my description of my personal development groups that many trainees were wary about what they said because they had to see their fellow trainees in other settings. If membership in a personal development group is to be a mandatory training experience, it would be more sensible if such groups were composed of students from different training courses so that each group member of a PDG would only meet with other members in the PDG setting. The practice of putting trainees in patient groups addresses this issue, but raises a number of other issues, a discussion of which is beyond the scope of the present chapter. My suggested alternative would also mean that trainees who had previously attended a PDG would not be obligated to attend another. If this practice had been in operation when I did my training I would have been spared three tedious years of attending PDG groups and would only have had to put up with one such year!

Preparing for a mid-life crisis that never happened: two months of Jungian therapy

As I approached my 40th birthday, I decided to re-enter personal therapy to prepare for my mid-life crisis. I should say that I wasn't experiencing a crisis at the time, nor have I subsequently had the crisis, but I was persuaded by the idea that preparing oneself adequately for a crisis is better psychologically than responding to that crisis after it happens. This time I deliberately chose a Jungian therapist on the basis that Jung's work seemed especially suited to mid-life issues and I wanted to see a female therapist merely because all my previous therapists had been male.

I remained in this therapy for about two months. It became clear to me fairly quickly and, I believe, also to my therapist that I was not suited to a Jungian approach. For one thing, I couldn't remember any of my dreams, which I think my therapist found somewhat frustrating, since it seemed to me that she liked to work with dreams. In addition, I found talking more helpful than her interventions which, to some degree, took me away from my train of thought, but not in a productive way. So I decided to terminate, an ending which was mutually agreed, well planned and amicable. This ending enabled us to work together on a collegial, professional level much later. These contacts revealed her to be much warmer and more humorous than she ever was as my therapist!

Comments
When I first entered individual therapy, I had just begun to train as a counsellor and therefore it could have been said that I was naïve in deciding to go into psychoanalytic therapy. My knowledge of what was available in the therapeutic scene was fairly limited and my major preoccupation was to find a therapist who came highly recommended. However, sixteen or so years on, I could not be said to be naïve. I had already had a good deal of therapy and had discovered that I was more suited to a cognitive-behavioural approach than a psychoanalytic one. So, you may be wondering: what possessed me to go into Jungian therapy? I have already given one explanation: Jung's approach was said to be particularly suited for those wishing to explore mid-life conflicts and although I hadn't begun to be affected by such issues, I was taking preventative measures. I also wanted to see a woman.

But as I have engaged in writing this chapter, it is also clearer to me that I would not have made a very good client of cognitive-behaviour therapy either, not in the early 1990s at any rate. If I had sought help from a cognitive-behaviour therapist at this point, I would have had to curb my tendency (which, as I write, I see would have been clearly present) to supervise my therapist. If I may humbly say so, I have been a leading proponent of REBT in particular, and of cognitive behaviour therapy in general, for a number of years and had obtained by the early 1990s a reputation in the field. I was probably Britain's leading REBT therapist and could not envisage consulting one of the very small band of trained British REBT therapists. First, I knew them all quite well and had trained most of them, and second, I would have been sorely tempted to supervise them and correct their errors! In addition, I would not have thought of consulting a more generic CBT therapist because they would not have focused on my irrational beliefs, but chosen instead to focus on my cognitive distortions and the like which I would have found frustrating as I did when I trained in Beck's cognitive therapy in 1981 after I had trained as an REBT therapist a few years earlier.

So it is a bit rich of me to criticise my Jungian therapist for practising an approach which I must have known in my heart of hearts I would not resonate with. This, of course, turned out to be the case and thus, I do not feel inclined to be too critical of my Jungian therapist.

I will only comment on one further thing. As I mentioned earlier, years after this therapy had ended, I met my ex-therapist in a professional activity and found her to be a charming, warm woman with a good sense of humour. These qualities were not apparent to me when I was her patient. This raises for me an interesting question. In adopting a fairly neutral therapeutic style, do psychodynamic therapists (and I include Jungians here), lose much of the therapeutic potency of their natural interpersonal style and qualities? My experience is that they probably do.

Consulting with Albert Ellis
The final personal 'therapy' experience concerns the consultations that I have had over the years with Albert Ellis, the founder of REBT and the person I most consider a mentor. For over twenty years I have made annual visits to what is now known as the Albert Ellis Institute in New York City. Whenever I go, I arrange to see Albert Ellis in what are known as his lunch time and supper time sessions. These are, in effect, his breaks between therapy sessions. While for the most part I have used these sessions to discuss matters relating to (a) finer points of the theory and practice of REBT; (b) problems that I have had in my clinical practice of REBT; and (c) joint writing projects, I have on various occasions used these sessions to consult with Al on a number of personal issues. Normally, these have been issues where I have failed to identify a subtle factor which has eluded me and thus I have not been able to get to the heart of the matter. Invariably, Al has helped me to identify this factor and has trusted me to take remedial steps to deal with the clarified problem on my own.

Comments
Of all the therapist-delivered treatment I have had — and when I put together all of them, I am shocked to learn how much therapy I have had (with so little return!) — Albert Ellis, in the sporadic times when I have discussed a personal issue with him, has been by far the best therapist I have ever had. Why is this so? First, our therapeutic discussions over the years have been in the context of him being more of a mentor than a therapist. This for me challenges the wisdom of implementing overly strict boundaries between therapy and non-therapy discussions with the same person. Such boundaries would be constructive for some, but not for me.

Another aspect of therapy with Al Ellis that I appreciated was his use of self-disclosure. I would discuss a personal issue with Al and he would tell me about a relevant experience that he had had with the same issue. Sometimes, he would tell me how he helped one of his clients with a similar problem. Rarely, if ever, would he practise formal, active-directive REBT with me. While I have never discussed this point with him, my sense is that he was quite aware that I knew REBT theory and practice very well and could trust that I had tried to use it with myself before discussing the issue with him. He respected my position as a knowledgeable REBT therapist, and sought to help me in ways that I had perhaps not thought of. His indirect approach here was most beneficial.

As I write this, I am reminded of a remark that one of my REBT colleagues made of supervisory feedback he had received on one of his therapy tapes by an REBT supervisor he had sought help from. 'He treated me as if I knew nothing about REBT,' claimed my colleague, who found this approach to supervision patronising and unhelpful. Al Ellis never once treated me in our therapeutic discussions as if I did not know REBT.

The other helpful aspect of having 'therapy' with Ellis was that his style with me did not change according to the issue we were discussing. I contrast this with the discrepancy between my Jungian therapist's 'inside therapy' style and her 'outside therapy' style. Al was his humorous, raunchy, interesting self no matter what we were discussing. In a phrase, I experienced him to be genuine in all his dealings with me, and this 'genuine informality' is a therapist quality that I find particularly helpful as a client and which I strive to achieve in my own work. I contrast this with the 'non-genuine formal' style of my other therapists.

It is fitting to close this chapter with my therapy experiences with Albert Ellis since I owe him so much as a professional. It is also fitting that I have ended with a discussion of my one positive therapist-delivered treatment that I have had. Although I have been critical of my previous therapists (with the exception of Albert Ellis), I want to end by saying that I would not be a very easy client for most therapists. I have a clear idea of what is helpful to me and what is not, and I have a definite preference for self-help, which makes being in therapy a problematic experience for me if that therapy is not focused sharply on encouraging me to help myself.

And yet, so many of my therapists failed to discover this. As a result I have learned to consistently ask myself whether or not my REBT practice best suits the needs of the person who is seeking my help. If it does, then we can proceed; but if not, I am prepared to refer this person to someone else. This is the lasting legacy of my personal therapy experiences and one that helps to keep my feet on the ground and helps me to remain dedicated and humble.

References

Bordin, E. S. (1979). The generalizability of the psychoanalytic concept of the working alliance. *Psychotherapy, Theory, Research and Practice, 16*, 252–60.

Dryden, W. (1991). *'It Depends': A Dialogue with Arnold Lazarus.* Buckingham: Open University Press.

Dryden, W. (1999a). *How to Accept Yourself.* London: Sheldon Press.

Dryden, W. (1999b). Friend or therapist? In S. Greenfield (ed.), *Therapy on the Couch: A Shrinking Future?* London: Camden Press.

Ellis, A. & Harper, R. A. (1975). *A New Guide to Rational Living.* Hollywood, CA: Wilshire.

Rogers, C. R. (1957). The necessary and sufficient conditions of therapeutic personality change. *Journal of Consulting Psychology, 21*, 95–103.

3

my idiosyncratic practice of REBT

In this chapter, I concentrate on my idiosyncratic practice of REBT and outline the reasons why I practise it in the way that I do. In particular, I discuss the importance of:

i. developing relationships with clients based on the principle of 'informed allies';

ii. developing a 'case conceptualisation' with complex 'cases';

iii. developing an REBT-influenced problems and goals list with clients;

iv. working with specific examples of target problems at the beginning of therapy;

v. identifying the critical 'A' in the assessment process;

vi. focusing on thinking 'Cs' as well as emotional and behavioural 'Cs';

vii. helping clients to develop and rehearse the full version of rational beliefs;

viii. encouraging clients to voice their doubts, reservations and objections to REBT concepts and to the REBT therapeutic process;

ix. deliberately instructing clients in the skills of REBT;

x. encouraging clients to take responsibility for their change process;

xi. using vivid methods to promote change; and

xii. using humour to develop rapport and promote change.

While this list of modes of practice is not designed to be an exhaustive account of my REBT practice, it is meant to indicate what I particularly emphasise in with clients from an REBT perspective.

Introduction
To those outside the cognitive-behavioural therapeutic tradition, all CBT approaches appear the same. This, of course, is far from the truth and while CBT approaches share some important similarities,

they also differ from one another in other important ways (cf. Dobson, 2001). For example, while REBT is similar to Beck's cognitive therapy in some respects, it differs from it in others (Dryden, 1984; Haaga & Davison, 1991).

When we consider a specific CBT approach like REBT are we on safe ground in assuming that all REBT therapists practise REBT in the same way? The answer is: it depends. Thus, Robb, Backx & Thomas (1999) found in their survey sample of REBT therapists on the Albert Ellis Institute referral list that when faced with clients who articulated the insight problem (i.e. 'It makes sense, but I don't really believe it yet'), therapists generally responded with cognitive interventions. Warren & McLellarn (1987), in their earlier survey of the same listed therapists, found that 'most RE[B]T therapists follow the philosophies and practices of RE[B]T as espoused and advocated by Ellis' (p.71). However, they also found that a 'significant number of therapists disagree with Ellis in some of his philosophical views and appeared to adapt the practice of RE[B]T to their own preferred style' (p.71). On the latter point, Warren & McLellarn found that 36% of their sample reported using irrational belief inventories as an assessment procedure; 56% reported using rational role reversal with 38% of clients; and 46% suggest that their clients (38%) listen to audiotapes of therapy sessions as a homework assignment.

Given that REBT therapists do seem to practise REBT in different ways, while at the same time concurring on some of its main theories and practices, we need to know more about individual differences among REBT practitioners. In this chapter, then, I will take the lead and outline my own practice of REBT, focusing particularly on what I emphasise in my practice and why I do so. Space considerations mean that I am unable to discuss any of these points in depth and I will rarely have an opportunity to detail *how* I make the interventions I discuss (see Dryden, 1999; Dryden, Neenan & Yankura, 1999 for a more detailed discussion on these points).

Developing relationships with clients based on the principle of 'informed allies'

Although REBT employs a variety of cognitive, emotive, imaginal and behavioural techniques (Ellis & Dryden, 1997), it needs to be stressed that these techniques are used within the context of a thera-peutic relationship and as such the development, maintenance and ending of this relationship needs to be considered. It is my view that the REBT literature has tended to underplay the importance of this relationship, a trend that I have tried to counterbalance in some of my own writings (Dryden, 1999; Dryden, 2001). In these writings and in my own practice of REBT, I emphasise a concept that I have called the principle of 'informed allies'. This concept comprises the principle of 'informed consent' and the tri-partite idea of the working alliance first introduced by Bordin (1979), which I first introduced into the REBT literature in the late 1980s (Dryden, 1987). Bordin's conceptualisation of the working alliance highlights the therapeutic bond that develops between therapist and client, the *goals* of the enterprise and the therapeutic tasks that therapist and client undertake during the life of the therapeutic relationship to facilitate goal attainment.

I operationalise the 'informed allies' concept in my practice of REBT in the following ways:

i. Early on in therapy, I outline the REBT model of psychological disturbance and psychological change to my client in bite-sized chunks to facilitate client understanding, using when appropriate the client's presenting problems. I also give them an idea of how I practise REBT and what this means for their participation in this process. I then ask them if they give their *informed consent* to proceed. Three outcomes are possible:
    (a) the client wishes to proceed, so we do;
    (b) the client is unsure. Here I usually offer a short-term contract so that the client can experience REBT in action and thus make a more informed decision to proceed or not; and
    (c) the client does not wish to proceed. Here I attempt to discover what therapeutic approach may 'fit' the client better and effect a suitable referral.

ii. In practising REBT I attempt to develop a suitable *bond* with my client. There are a number of issues that I keep in mind in doing so:
    (a) *Informal vs. formal.* Clients differ with respect to their wishes for an informal or formal relationship with their therapists. As long as these wishes are healthy and do not unwittingly perpetuate the clients' problems, I am happy to meet their preferences on this point.
    (b) *Directiveness.* While REBT is an active-directive, persuasive approach to therapy, I tend to be less directive and less overtly persuasive with clients who are reactant in personality organisation and who react adversely to attempts to influence them. With these clients I am explicit about REBT concepts and emphasise their choice concerning whether or not they implement these concepts in their life.

(c) *Humour.* Clients differ widely concerning their response to humorous interventions in REBT. While I prefer to practise REBT with a sense of humour (see below), I am quite happy to practise REBT in a more serious vein when this is required. I often have an intuitive 'feel' concerning a client's 'humour quotient', but when I am unsure about whether or not a client will respond well to my brand of humour, I offer 'trial' jokes (in the same way that an analyst makes trial interpretations) and gauge his or her response to these. I also ask for feedback on my humour and adjust my therapeutic style according to the feedback I receive.

iii. In my experience as a supervisor of trainee REBT therapists, I often find that trainees lose sight of their clients' *goals* as they work with their clients over time (Neenan & Dryden, 2001). I am mindful in my own practice to keep my focus and that of my clients on their goals for change. In doing so, I consider that I am being a good role model since one of the ways in which clients maintain their psychological problems is lack of mindfulness about their healthy goals. I will discuss goals further later in this chapter.

iv. I mentioned earlier that the technical aspects of REBT are often highlighted in the literature. From a working alliance perspective, I am particularly concerned about the following issues concerning therapeutic *tasks:*

(a) that clients understand (i) what their tasks are; (ii) what my tasks are as an REBT therapist and (iii) the relationship between both sets of tasks;

(b) that clients understand the relationship between their therapeutic tasks and their therapeutic goals;

(c) that clients are deemed capable of executing their tasks before they are asked to carry them out;

(d) that clients are trained to carry out their therapeutic tasks as appropriate;

(e) that I carry out my therapeutic tasks with skill, care and enthusiasm; and

(f) that I suggest the use of therapeutic tasks that are potent enough to help clients to achieve their goals.

Developing a 'case formulation' with complex 'cases'
Beginning with the pioneering work of Persons (1989), cognitive therapists have espoused the value of carrying out case formulations to aid

therapeutic intervention. REBT therapists have not embraced this concept as readily and indeed, my work on the subject is the only publication that centrally addresses this issue from an REBT perspective (Dryden, 1999). Indeed, when I showed a pre-publication copy of this work to Albert Ellis, he questioned the efficiency of making case formulations prior to therapeutic intervention in REBT. His point was that therapists can waste valuable therapeutic time making such formulations and that they could better use such time helping clients to address and overcome their psychological problems. This would be true if therapists carried out lengthy pre-treatment case formulations with all of their clients, but I am not suggesting this, nor is it my practice. My view about conducting a case formulation is this. I will do one when:

i. *The referral is a complex one.* Once the client has given their informed consent to proceed with REBT and if it transpires that the client has complex problems, I will carry out a full case formulation before making any substantive change-based interventions since doing so will help me to understand the complexity of the client's 'case' and help me to save time in the longer run. This meets Ellis's inefficiency argument.

ii. *The client isn't making progress as anticipated and/or I am stuck with the client.* When I predict that I can help a client, but the client doesn't make the anticipated progress or I get stuck and don't know why, I will then tend to do a full case formulation with that person. This often helps me to understand why the client isn't making the anticipated progress and/or why I am stuck and suggests avenues for intervention that had not previously occurred to me.

Let me now briefly describe the factors that I consider when I do a formal case formulation. I call this doing a 'UPCP' which stands for 'Understanding the Person in the Context of his/her Problems' because I do not like referring to a person as a 'case' (Dryden, 1999). This involves:

i. obtaining basic information and utilising initial impressions;

ii. developing a problem list;

iii. identifying goals for therapy;

iv. developing a list of problem emotions ('Cs');

v. developing a list of problem critical 'As';

vi. identifying core irrational beliefs;

vii. identifying dysfunctional behavioural 'Cs';

viii. identifying the purposive nature of dysfunctional behaviour;

ix. identifying ways in which the client prevents or cuts short the experience of problems;

x. identifying ways in which the client compensates for problems;

xi. identifying mctapsychological problems;

xii. identifying the cognitive consequences of core irrational beliefs;

xiii. identifying the manner of problem expression and the interpersonal responses to these expressions;

xiv. identifying the client's health and medication status;

xv. developing an understanding of relevant predisposing factors;

xvi. predicting the client's likely responses to therapy;

xvii. negotiating a narrative account of the UPCP for consideration with the client.

For more detailed information on how to conduct a UPCP together with a case example see chapter 5 in Dryden (1999).

The final point that I wish to make on 'case formulations' is one that Ellis has made informally in many of his professional workshops. This is that competent REBT practitioners build up a working picture of their clients as they proceed in therapy and share this with their clients as a way of fine tuning these more informal case formulations. Albert Ellis is very good at this, as those who have witnessed him conducting therapy or been supervised by him will testify, but he has not written on this subject to any significant degree and this aspect of REBT has tended to be neglected.

Developing an REBT-influenced 'problems and goals' list with clients

As I listed above, conducting a problem and goals list with clients is an important component of a 'UPCP' or REBT 'case' formulation. It is my practice to develop such a list with virtually all of my clients (and not just when I am conducting a 'UPCP') since this helps both of us to keep on track throughout the therapeutic process. This is probably common practice among REBT therapists. What may be different is the way in which I do this.

Rather than ask my clients to develop a problems and goals list in their own way, I encourage them to use an REBT-inspired formula in doing so (Dryden, 2001). Usually, I help them to use this formula in a session and then once they have understood it, I suggest that they complete it as a homework assignment. I will now provide this formula and illustrate its use with a client example.

Formula for specifying a problem
Problem = Type of situation + inferential theme + unhealthy negative emotion + unconstructive behaviour/subsequent unrealistic thinking.

Example of specified problem
Whenever my boss asks to see me (type of situation), I think he is going to criticise me (inferential theme) and I feel anxious about this (unhealthy negative emotion). I deal with this anxiety by overworking so that he has nothing to criticise me for (unconstructive behaviour).

In helping clients to set goals, I encourage them in the first instance to keep the type of situation and the inferential theme the same and change the remaining factors. In doing so, I am being consistent with the traditional REBT approach which states that it is important at the outset *not* to change 'A' until clients have achieved a fair measure of change at 'B'. Following the tradition set by Wessler & Wessler (1980), 'A' here incorporates the situation and the inference about the situation.

Formula for specifying a goal
Goal = Type of situation + inferential theme + healthy negative emotion (*rather than* the unhealthy negative emotion) + constructive behaviour/subsequent realistic thinking (*rather than* the unconstructive behaviour/subsequent unrealistic thinking).

Example of specified goal
Whenever my boss asks to see me (type of situation) and I think he is going to criticise me (inferential theme), I want to feel concerned about this (healthy negative emotion) *rather than* anxious. I want to

deal with this situation by doing the same level of work as if things were going well (constructive behaviour) *rather than* overworking.

Note that in the goal formula and example that I encourage clients to specify their healthy emotional, behavioural and/or thinking goals as well as what they are going to strive not to feel, act and/or think; hence the emphasis on the phrase '*rather than*' in both formula and example.

I also help clients to distinguish between overcoming psychological problem (OPP) goals and personal development (PD) goals and to set both if relevant. Since this issue is outside the scope of this chapter, I refer interested readers to Dryden (2001).

Focusing on specific examples of target problems at the beginning of therapy and working them through

In my view, one of the most common errors that trainee REBT therapists make at the beginning of the REBT therapeutic process is to work with clients at an abstract, non-specific level rather than at a specific level (Neenan & Dryden, 2001). Of course, I endeavour to avoid making this error whenever I can. I do so by encouraging clients to identify a problem from their problem list that they would like to work on. The selected problem is known as the 'target problem'. Then I encourage clients to identify a specific example of this target problem that we can work on and I explain why it is important for us to remain with this example and work it through. I explain that people make themselves disturbed in specific situations or when imagining specific situations and that given this, working with a specific example of their target problem will help us both to identify key elements of the ABC framework.

Thus, working with a specific example helps clients to identify with greater clarity than would be the case when working with abstract examples:

i. the aspect of the situation (actual or inferred) they particularly disturbed themselves about (known as the 'critical A' — see below);

ii. their primary unhealthy negative emotion (emotional 'C');

iii. their unconstructive behaviours or behavioural impulses (behavioural 'C'); and

iv. their subsequent distorted thinking (cognitive 'C').

I then encourage my clients to stay with this specific example until I have helped them to identify, challenge and change the specific irrational beliefs that they held in this situation, and encourage them to imagine themselves responding to the critical 'A' while holding their specific rational beliefs and while acting constructively and thinking realistically. Finally, I encourage them to practise their rational beliefs and associated constructive behaviour and realistic thinking while facing the situation at 'A' which contains the inferential theme under consideration. When clients have done this, I help them to capitalise on their progress by encouraging them to generalise their learning to other relevant specific situations. Finally, I contend that working with specific examples of target problems helps guard against REBT becoming an overly intellectualised enterprise which it can easily become if the therapist works with the client at a general, abstract level.

Identifying the critical 'A' in the assessment process
In REBT theory, the concept of 'A' (or activating event) is deceptively simple. As its name implies, it is an event that activates something. Now, of course, it does not activate the person's emotional, behavioural and thinking responses at 'C' because that would be antithetical to REBT's ABC model of psychological disturbance and health. Rather, 'A' activates the person's belief and it is this 'A' x 'B' interaction that accounts for the person's psychological responses at 'C'. However, what actually constitutes an 'A'? This is where the distinction between an actual event and an inference about that event becomes salient. One point is important here: Ellis could have used 'A' to refer to an actual event, but he didn't. He clearly uses the term 'activating' when referring to 'A'.

To complicate matters a little further, some of us now use the term 'critical 'A'' (Dryden, 1995) to denote the core component of a situation that actually triggers the person's beliefs at 'B'. In using this term we recognise that there are many possible 'As' in a situation, but only one triggers a belief which accounts for a particular emotional-behavioural-cognitive response at 'C'. To make life even more complex for the REBT therapist, a client can experience several emotions in what Wessler & Wessler (1980) have called an emotional episode — an episode in which the client experiences emotions (and, I would add, behaviours and thinking responses as well) — and that each of these emotions are triggered by its own set of beliefs about a different critical 'A'.

When 'As' are inferential they have recurring themes when paired with different emotions. This was noted over 25 years ago by Beck (1976), whose thinking on this point has had a decided effect on my own with respect to the nature and role that 'As' play in the ABC model. For instance, when a client reports anxiety, look for the inferential theme of threat or danger in their report; when depression is reported look for loss or failure, etc. (see Dryden, 1995 for an extended discussion of this issue).

In my view and experience, critical 'As' are often inferential in nature. Given this, in identifying the critical 'A' in a specific ABC I often merge the actual with the specified inferential theme in the client's account (e.g. 'I was most anxious about my girlfriend looking over my shoulder' (actual situation) 'in case she found someone else more attractive than me' (inferential theme).

I have devised a number of different ways of identifying critical 'As' (see Dryden, 1995) and now see the importance of distinguishing between inferences at 'A' and inferences at 'C' (see below). Thus, my practice of REBT features an emphasis on helping the client and myself to identify and work with the critical 'A' in any highlighted emotional episode. This can often be a complex procedure and one which novice REBT therapists struggle to do well and succinctly.

Focusing on thinking 'Cs' as well as emotional and behavioural 'Cs'

I mentioned above that inferences can occur both at 'A' and at 'C' in the ABC framework. When inferences occur at 'C' in this framework they denote the fact that beliefs can not only have emotional and behavioural consequences, but thinking consequences as well. There are a variety of ways of dealing with thinking consequences in REBT. Thus, one can:

i.   deal with them as 'As' rather than as 'Cs' (e.g. as activating events for a subsequent ABC: let's suppose that everybody in the room does laugh at you, now how would you feel about that? Or as inferences as part of an inference chain: and if everybody in the room does laugh at you, what, for you, would be anxiety-provoking about that?);

ii.   challenge their distorted nature (e.g. 'What is the likelihood that everybody in the room will laugh at you?'); or

iii.   educate clients about how they create them and to use them to identify the ABC in which they occur as a 'C'.

I find that while I do, at times, use the first two strategies listed above, I increasingly use the third strategy. Thus, if a client says that she is scared of speaking in public because she fears that everybody in the room will laugh at her, I show the client how they create this distorted inferential 'C'. I ask her questions such as 'what would have to happen for you not to fear that everyone in the room will laugh at you?' If she says: 'For me to have a sense of confidence about what I am talking about', I will show her that the opposite of this is likely to be her critical 'A' and teach her how she creates the aforementioned thinking 'C' by using the ABC framework. Thus:

'A' = Not being confident about what I will be talking about to a group

'B' = I must be confident about what I am talking about and it is terrible if I'm not

'C' emotional = anxiety
behavioural = urge to cancel the talk
thinking = 'If I give the talk everybody will laugh at me'

Helping this client to dispute the irrational belief in the above example means that it is far less likely that she will create the thinking 'C' than if the irrational belief remains unchallenged. If the thinking 'C' persists then it can be dealt with by using the other two strategies listed above.

Finally, I want to note that it is a feature of my practice of REBT that I train my clients to identify the cognitive distortions in their inferential thinking so that they can treat these distorted inferences as thinking 'Cs' rather than to challenge them as distorted inferences as cognitive therapists are more likely to do. In this way, my practice of REBT differs from the practice of cognitive therapy.

Helping clients to develop and rehearse the full version of rational beliefs

As is well known, according to the REBT theory of psychological disturbance and health, irrational beliefs are at the core of the former and rational beliefs are at the core of the latter. Consequently, it is a major task of REBT therapists to help their clients to identify, challenge and change their irrational beliefs and to replace them with rational beliefs which need to be rehearsed and acted on sufficiently often if they are to make a significant difference in the clients' emotional lives. So far, what I have said would feature in the practice of virtually all REBT therapists. What characterises my practice that might not be sufficiently present in the therapeutic work of my colleagues is the emphasis that I place on what I call full versions of rational beliefs.

As I have noted elsewhere (Neenan & Dryden, 1999), a rational belief normally has two components: one that asserts the presence of the partial rational belief and the other that negates the presence of the irrational belief. Thus, if my client holds the following demand: 'I must do well in my examination', I help him, in this case, to develop and rehearse the following alternative full preference: 'I want to do well in my examination (asserted partial preference), but I do not have to do so (negated demand)'. I strive to do this consistently with all forms of rational beliefs (full preferences, full anti-awfulising beliefs, full HFT beliefs and full acceptance beliefs). I have found that when I do so my client is less likely to transmute her rational beliefs back into irrational beliefs than when I work with the partial versions of rational beliefs (e.g. I want to do well in my examination) (Dryden, 2001).

Encouraging clients to voice their doubts, reservations and objections to REBT concepts and to the REBT therapeutic process
One of the major features of REBT is that it has an explicit model of how people disturb themselves and what they need to do to undisturb themselves. Another major feature of this therapeutic approach is that it endeavours to teach this model to clients whenever possible and whenever appropriate. It is a feature of my practice to encourage clients to voice doubts, reservations and objections they have to any of the REBT concepts that I am teaching them or to any aspect of the REBT therapeutic process. My clinical experience has been that clients frequently harbour such doubts etc. and if these are not brought to light and examined with clients then they will have a decided negative influence on the therapeutic process. I have found it to be especially important to communicate to clients that I am very open to having REBT criticised in this way and to respond to these criticisms in a non-defensive manner. I also compliment clients for speaking their mind, which is, I have found, a good strategy for unearthing further doubts etc. later in the therapeutic process. Common doubts are too numerous to list here (see Dryden, 1995, 2001), but a few examples will suffice:

- acceptance means resignation
- accepting others means condoning their behaviour
- musts are motivating
- because preferences allow failure, they make it more likely that failure will occur. Musts, on the other hand, because they don't permit failure make failure less likely to occur
- REBT is simplistic
- REBT is brainwashing.

From this illustrative list, the deleterious effect of such doubts on the practice of REBT can be clearly seen and reinforces the importance of encouraging clients to reveal their doubts etc. and the importance of dealing with them in a sensitive but authoritative manner.

Deliberately instructing clients in the skills of REBT

I have always remembered a comment that Maxie C. Maultsby Jr. made at the very first workshop on REBT that I attended in 1977. He said that in essence effective therapy is self-therapy. In other words, clients will benefit from psychotherapy to the extent that they apply the principles of the therapeutic approach in their own lives. This fits very well with an educationally oriented approach such as REBT and over the years I have elaborated this concept to the point that I have recently published a book entitled *Reason to Change: A Rational Emotive Behaviour Therapy (REBT) Workbook* (Dryden, 2001). While this is a self-help workbook, I use the material with my clients since it gives step-by-step guidance with examples on how to use some of the major REBT techniques. My practice is to devote a portion of each therapy session to the work that clients have done between sessions on the workbook and the rest of the session on clients' target problems. In this way, I can monitor the progress that my clients are making on their problems and on their REBT skill development.

Of course, not all clients take to the skills development emphasis of the *Reason to Change* workbook and thus flexibility is the watchword here (as elsewhere). With such clients, I suggest that they do not use the workbook at all and I take a non-workbook approach with them. However, I deliberately instruct most of my clients in the use of core REBT skills and therefore this is an identifiable and key aspect of my practice of REBT.

Encouraging clients to take responsibility for change

Deliberately instructing clients in the skills in REBT is part of a wider emphasis that I place on encouraging clients to take responsibility for change. Thus, at the outset I outline my tasks as an REBT therapist and their tasks as REBT clients (Dryden, 1995). These are basically as follows:

- specify problems
- be open to the therapist's REBT framework
- apply the specific principle of emotional responsibility (i.e. acknowledge and act on the idea that I largely make myself disturbed by the holding a set of irrational beliefs

- apply the principle of therapeutic responsibility (i.e. acknowledge and act on the idea that in order to undisturb myself I need to dispute my irrational beliefs, rehearse and deepen my conviction in my rational beliefs and act and think in ways that are consistent with these developing rational beliefs and that I commit myself to doing this regularly)
- disclose doubts, difficulties and obstacles to change.

In addition, I ask my clients, also at the outset of the therapeutic process, how much time they are willing to devote to helping themselves *per day*. I point out to them that the best predictor of progress in the cognitive therapies is the regular completion of homework assignments.

Throughout therapy, I remind clients that I don't expect them to do my job and I am not able to do theirs. Once again, I want to stress that this emphasis on client responsibility for change is modified according to the client's present capability for taking such responsibility.

Using vivid methods to promote change

In the early 1980s, I published a series of papers (collated in Dryden, 1986) on what I called vivid RE[B]T. Vivid interventions are those that bring the therapeutic process to life and I argued then as I still do now that such interventions instigate change more effectively than non-vivid interventions. A good example of this is vivid representations of 'As' where such 'As' are presented in clear and emotionally impactful ways, enabling clients' beliefs and feelings to be evoked and worked with in therapy sessions.

Thus, my work is still characterised by the use of such methods and I apply the same caveats as I described in the 1986 compilation [e.g. don't overuse vivid interventions in therapy sessions, don't use them with clients with a tendency towards a histrionic response and when you use them with clients use intellectualisation as a defence, introduce such methods gradually and at an initial 'low dose' of vividness, increasing this 'dose' if such clients respond well to the initial 'dose' (see Dryden, 1986 for a fuller discussion of vivid REBT).]

Using humour to develop rapport and promote change

The final distinguishing feature of my REBT practice that I want to discuss is my use of humour to develop rapport and to promote change. Although I mentioned the use of humour in the first mode of practice that I discussed in this chapter, I wanted to include it separately since it is such a defining characteristic of my work.

I find it difficult to describe my use of humour in REBT. It is something that one has to observe to understand. However, it is a combination of puns, witticisms, bringing together disparate aspects of a client's experience in humorous fusion, self-mocking and jokes. I don't, on the other hand, make much use of rational humorous songs (Ellis, 1987). Now, I don't want you to get the idea that my sessions are full of humour since this is not the case: I am serious when I need to be and often. However, I have found that my humorous interventions do lighten the therapeutic atmosphere to good effect, particularly in REBT group therapy. My experience is that humour is a therapeutic factor in that it helps clients to take themselves seriously, but not too seriously. It also serves to remind clients of a therapeutic point between sessions. My clients are wont to say that one of my humorous remarks came into their mind at an appropriate time and reminded them of a salient REBT concept that they were then able to translate into practice. In this sense, humour can also be seen as a vivid intervention.

I hope that I have conveyed in this chapter my idiosyncratic practice of REBT and that this encourages other REBT therapists to discuss their own particular way of practising REBT.

References

Beck, A. T. (1976). *Cognitive Therapy and the Emotional Disorders.* New York: International Universities Press.

Bordin, E. S. (1979). The generalizability of the concept of the working alliance. *Psychotherapy: Theory, Research and Practice, 16,* 252–60.

Dobson, K. S. (ed.) (2001). *Handbook of Cognitive-Behavioral Therapies,* 2nd edn. New York: Guilford.

Dryden, W. (1984). Rational-emotive therapy and cognitive therapy: A critical comparison. In M. A. Reda & M. J. Mahoney (eds.), *Cognitive Psychotherapies: Recent Developments in Theory, Research and Practice* (pp. 81–99). Cambridge, MA: Ballinger.

Dryden, W. (1986). Vivid methods in rational-emotive therapy. In A. Ellis & R. Grieger (eds.), *Handbook of Rational-Emotive Therapy, Volume 2* (pp. 221–45). New York: Springer.

Dryden, W. (1987). The therapeutic alliance in rational-emotive individual therapy. In W. Dryden, *Current Issues in Rational-Emotive Therapy* (pp. 59–71). London: Croom Helm.

Dryden, W. (1995). *Preparing for Client Change in Rational Emotive Behaviour Therapy.* London: Whurr.

Dryden, W. (1999). *Rational Emotive Behaviour Therapy: A Personal Approach.* Bicester, Oxon: Winslow Press.

Dryden, W. (2001). *Reason to Change: A Rational Emotive Behav-*

iour Therapy (REBT) Workbook. London: Brunner/Routledge.

Dryden, W., Neenan, M. & Yankura, J. (1999). *Counselling Individuals: A Rational Emotive Behavioural Handbook,* third edition. London: Whurr.

Ellis, A. (1987). The use of rational humorous songs in psychotherapy. In W. F. Fry & W. A. Salameh (eds.), *Handbook of Humor in Psychotherapy: Advances in the Clinical Use of Humor.* Sarasota FL: Professional Resource Exchange.

Ellis, A. & Dryden, W. (1997). *The Practice of Rational Emotive Behavior Therapy,* second edition. New York: Springer.

Haaga, D. A. F. & Davison, G. C. (1991). Disappearing differences do not always reflect healthy integration: An analysis of cognitive therapy and rational-emotive therapy. *Journal of Psychotherapy Integration, 1*(4), 287–303.

Neenan, M. & Dryden, W. (1999). *Rational Emotive Behaviour Therapy: Advances in Theory and Practice.* London: Whurr.

Neenan, M. & Dryden, W. (2001). *Learning from Errors in Rational Emotive Behaviour Therapy.* London: Whurr.

Persons, J. (1989). *Cognitive Therapy in Practice: A Case Formulation Approach.* New York: Norton.

Robb, H., Backx, W. & Thomas, J. (1999). The use of cognitive, emotive and behavioral interventions in rational emotive behavior therapy when clients lack 'emotional' insight. *Journal of Rational-Emotive & Cognitive-Behavior Therapy, 17*(3), 201–9.

Warren, R. & McLellarn, R. W. (1987). What do RET therapists think they are doing? *Journal of Rational-Emotive Therapy, 5*(2), 71–91.

Wessler, R. A. & Wessler, R. L. (1980). *The Principles and Practice of Rational-Emotive Therapy.* San Francisco: Jossey-Bass.

4

**hard-earned lessons
in counselling**

I became interested in counselling as a direct result of pursuing a PhD in social psychology. My topic was self-disclosure, and many of the papers I was reading at that time concerned self-disclosure in counselling. These articles awakened a powerful response in me, and this, together with my experiences of going to encounter groups in the late 1960s and early 1970s, led me to conclude that I wanted to become a counsellor.

My first major training was a one-year, full-time diploma in counselling in educational settings at Aston University. This course was basically a training in client-centred counselling, with some emphasis on behavioural techniques for specific problems such as examination anxiety.

For reasons that will become apparent later in this chapter, I came to the conclusion that I needed further training, and enrolled on a two-year, part-time course in psychodynamic psychotherapy. This was an introductory course, and served to convince me that this approach was not for me. During it I developed an interest in rational-emotive therapy (RET) and decided to pursue further training in this approach. This I did part-time from 1977 to 1980 at the Institute for RET in New York. At about the same time I studied for an MSc in psychotherapy at Warwick University with John and Marcia Davis. This eclectic course helped me to integrate some of my previously disparate training and practical experiences, and underscored for me that developing and maintaining a productive working alliance is a crucial ingredient in effective counselling and psychotherapy.

Subsequent training in Aaron Beck's cognitive therapy in Philadelphia, and Arnold Lazarus's multimodal therapy in Princeton, New Jersey extended my practice as an eclectically orientated counsellor, albeit one who is firmly in the rational-emotive and cognitive-behavioural tradition.

My experience of working with clients has been quite broad. I have worked with individuals in a university counselling service, a GP practice, a clinic which specialises in helping clients who are depressed, and a clinical psychology department. I have worked with couples in Relate, and with groups at the Institute for RET as Albert Ellis's co-therapist. I don't work with families when there are children or adolescents involved, because I believe this work requires special skills which I do not have. As you can imagine, all this training and experience has provided me with many opportunities to learn the hard way.

Thriving on variety
In April 1981 I went to Philadelphia to begin a six-month sabbatical at the Center for Cognitive Therapy. My intention was to gain a thorough

training, and to this end I resolved to restrict myself to clinical practice so that I was not distracted from my purpose. It is important to stress at this point that I had always had variety in my working life. My first and, at this juncture, only job was as lecturer in counselling at Aston University. My duties there were quite varied, and involved training and supervising counselling trainees, counselling students at the university's counselling service, administration, and academic writing/research. I had never counselled full-time — something I regarded as a lacuna in my career to date, and one I was keen to fill. There was something amiss, I reasoned, when someone whose main job was to train people to work as full-time counsellors had never worked as a full-time counsellor himself. So I was doubly enthusiastic — first, about immersing myself in an exciting, new approach to counselling, and second, about working as a practitioner. I would take a break from writing and recharge my batteries by refraining from any involvement in training and supervising activities. After all, wasn't that partly what constituted a sabbatical — a break from one's usual duties?

After an initial intensive training in the fundamentals of cognitive therapy, I was deemed to be competent enough to see clients at the Center, and as I had about six years' experience as a counsellor, I was given a reasonably heavy load of about twenty cases. I set off with considerable enthusiasm. I enjoyed the cases I was assigned, and revelled in the expert, one-to-one supervision I received. 'This is the life', I thought, and the idea that I had been missing something fundamental by not working as a full-time counsellor strengthened in my mind.

Then it happened. I began to feel increasingly restless and irritable for no apparent reason. Initially, I couldn't understand what these feelings pointed to, so I decided to apply some of the cognitive techniques I had recently learned and had been applying with my clients on myself, in the hope that this would shed some light on my puzzling experience. In particular, I decided to investigate my automatic thoughts, that is, those thoughts that would pop into my head automatically without any conscious intent. Here is a simple sample of those thoughts and how I responded to them:

I'm just not cut out to be a counsellor.
Response: That's not true. I've been seeing clients now for over six years, and I've never questioned my suitability before. I'm doing reasonably well with the clients with whom I'm working, so I don't think it's true that I'm not cut out to be a counsellor.

I'm not cut out to be a cognitive therapist.
Response: Well, it's true that I have some doubts about cognitive therapy. In lots of ways, I favour RET, which, although similar to cognitive therapy in many respects, is quite different in others. However, I don't think this explains the full extent of my restlessness and irritability, which was now quite marked.

There's something missing in my life.
Response: Now that seems far closer to the heart of the matter. I know there's nothing amiss in my personal life. I've just got married and have my lovely wife with me, so that's not it. However, I do feel there's something missing in my work. What am I not doing that I'm used to and that I enjoy?

It was when I asked myself this last question that the mist began to clear. I missed the other activities that constituted the varied nature of my work at Aston University. It was the variety that I was missing! Once the issue had become clear, the remedy was simple. First, I began to plan an academic paper that compared and contrasted RET with cognitive therapy (Dryden, 1984). Then, I made arrangements to fulfil the trainer and supervisor parts of myself by travelling weekly to the Institute for RET in New York to participate in their training programmes, and serve as one of their supervisors. I did all this while maintaining the same caseload at the Center for Cognitive Therapy.

What this experience taught me was that I thrive on variety in my work, and when this missing, I very quickly become unfulfilled with consequent feelings of restlessness and irritability. It was a profound learning experience, albeit a difficult one, and I have taken heed of it ever since.

The importance of being an 'authentic chameleon'
In 1981, Arnold Lazarus published a book entitled *The Practice of Multimodal Therapy,* in which he introduced the concept of the counsellor as 'authentic chameleon'. By this he meant that it is important for counsellors to vary their interpersonal style with different clients, but in an authentic manner. In the same year, and well before I had read Lazarus's book, I learned the hard way about the value of being an 'authentic chameleon'.

At the time that I learned this lesson I was working at the Center for Cognitive Therapy. I was assigned Ian, a forty-two-year-old man who was quite depressed. Early on in counselling he spoke about his previous therapists, but in a pejorative fashion. He complained they were 'a bunch of stuffed shirts', who acted very formally towards him and who sat behind their desks. 'Their dress reflected their manner', he went on, saying that it was as if they wore white coats, such was the interpersonal distance between them and him. In response to my question concerning the type of therapeutic relationship he was seeking, he said he was looking for someone with whom he could loosen up and 'rap'. His preferred image was of the two of us sitting with our feet up on the coffee table discussing his problems in a very informal way, or 'shooting the breeze' as he put it.

Now, I saw no good reason why I could not practise cognitive therapy in this way, and so week after week we would have our 'rap' sessions, as Ian came to call them, while I conceptualised my approach as informal cognitive therapy. I followed all the strategic and technical rules of the therapy, but did so while using a lot of self-disclosure, within a relationship which looked for all intents and purposes as two friends having a heart-to-heart discussion about the problems of one of them. We did indeed take to putting our feet up on the coffee table, and what is more we took turns bringing to the session cans of soda, which we consumed during the therapy hour. The outcome was a salubrious one, and at the end of our work together Ian pointed to our friendly, informal relationship as the most important therapeutic factor, from his vantage point.

Three weeks after I started seeing Ian, I was assigned Mrs G, a fifty-seven-year-old woman who had a considerable problem with anger over what were a number of minor environmental stressors. At our first session, she told me she was looking forward to meeting me because she always found Englishmen very correct and civilised, and fully expected me to observe the protocol of a professional relationship, unlike her previous therapist, who, she claimed, was overly friendly and who she sacked 'in very short order'.

Now, it should be noted that I saw Mrs G an hour before my session with Ian, and it was this temporal proximity that made life difficult for me, but which provided me with the learning that has stayed with me ever since. Every counsellor, I believe, has an interpersonal style which is natural to him or her, and mine was closer to the informality I demonstrated with Ian than to the stark formality demanded by Mrs G; and when I use the term 'demanded' I do so advisedly. For Mrs G reprimanded me for every slip into what she considered to be an inappropriately informal relationship. Before I fully learned my lesson, I made what proved to be the following errors with Mrs G, each of which met with a sharp rebuke: first, I once used her first name, to which she replied, 'Dr Dryden, will you please refrain from calling me by my Christian name'; second, I once tried to illustrate a therapeutic point by making a disclosure about my own similar experience, to which Mrs G replied, 'Dr Dryden, I am not paying the Center good money to hear about your personal problems'; and, third, I once greeted her at the beginning of the session without my jacket and tie, wrongly thinking (or perhaps hoping!) that I was seeing Ian; her reply was, 'Dr Dryden, will you please put on your jacket and tie.' Once I had fully digested the point, namely that I had to be strictly formal with Mrs G, we got on famously, and she made quite good headway overcoming the problems for which she sought therapy.

What I learned starkly was that different clients benefit from different types of bonds with their counsellor, and that if we are going to take seriously the point that clients are different, we need to acknowledge that one way in which they differ concerns their expectations of what is a helpful counsellor style. Furthermore, I learned that as long as the counsellor has that style in his or her repertoire, and can be authentic in adopting the style — which, importantly, should not reinforce the client's problems — then there is much to be gained by being an 'authentic chameleon'.

Different strokes for different folks
I have been influenced by the work of Ed Bordin (1979), who has written sensitively about the working alliance in counselling and psychotherapy. He argues that there are three major components of the alliance which need to be considered when appraising our counselling work with clients. These components are bonds, i.e., the relationship between counsellor and client and its vicissitudes; goals, i.e., the objectives that counsellor and client have concerning their work together; and tasks, i.e., the activities in which counsellor and client engage in their quest to help the client achieve his or her goals.

In the previous section I discussed the lesson I learned in the bond domain of the alliance. In this section I will discuss a similar lesson I learned in the task domain. In fact, I had to learn the lesson several times before I grasped its true message.

As I mentioned, I was originally trained in person-centred counselling. I remember being very enthusiastic about this approach when I was learning about it, and considered that I had found the key to helping people. My first clients responded well to this approach, and this early experience tended to reinforce my unitary view of the counselling universe. Eventually, however, an increasing number of my clients indicated that they wanted more from counselling than the empathy, respect, and genuineness I was offering them. For a time I thought the fault lay with me. The reason I wasn't helping these clients, I thought, was because I wasn't being empathic, respectful, or genuine enough. This view was in fact reinforced in supervision as my supervisor and I pored over my counselling tapes, looking for instances of my inaccurate empathy.

I remember one case in particular when my client and I struggled for weeks until I broke ranks and, taking a leaf out of Albert Ellis's book, I successfully helped the client by strongly attacking her rigidly held belief that she needed approval in order to be happy. This case proved to be one of the influences that led me to go New York to train in RET.

Again I thought I had found the Holy Grail. It was clear to me that all clients held irrational beliefs, and therefore my task was clear — to help them to identify, challenge, and change these beliefs using a host of cognitive, emotive, and behavioural techniques. Indeed, I had a lot of success using RET. However, not all clients responded well to this approach.

So how did I initially deal with these expectations? I did what people tend to do when faced with potentially threatening information: I denied it, or I distorted it to protect my unitary view. So the client who kept claiming I was not listening to her closely enough was labelled, I hate to admit it now, a 'resistant client'; the man who wanted to talk at length about his childhood experiences at boarding school was given the standard RET line that it was his present beliefs about these experiences that were the real root of his problem, and if only he would change these then all would be well. A third example of my failure in the task domain of the alliance occurred early in my career when through lack of knowledge I omitted to employ a variant of response prevention with a client with a handwashing compulsion — a task which the research literature clearly demonstrates is indicated for this type of problem. In my naivety, I once again thought that empathy, etc., was all-powerful.

It took quite a bit of disconfirming evidence to disabuse me of my unitary view of the counselling universe. I now believe that different clients need to perform different tasks in counselling at different points in the process. If this idea is correct, then I, as a counsellor, need to be proficient in a wide variety of counselling tasks myself, or refer the client to someone who is better equipped to help them — an issue I take up in my next hard-earned lesson.

Does this mean I am no longer a rational-emotive counsellor? Well, yes and no. I still use rational-emotive theory as a core theoretical framework; however, I am much broader in my use of counselling tasks than I used to be, and much more receptive to my clients' views of what will be of value to them in the counselling process. In short, I now have a pluralistic view of counselling rather than a unitary one.

I may not be the best person to help

In my early days as a counsellor, I fluctuated between thinking I had discovered the answer to all clients' problems, to feeling quite uncertain about my ability to help anyone. One way I compensated for the latter was to believe I had to take on anyone who came to me for help. The idea that I might not be the best person to counsel someone was so threatening that the thought rarely, if ever, entered my mind.

Fortunately, I had several experiences with clients that led me to revise this view. One example which stands out in my mind occurred when I lived and worked in Birmingham. I was fairly well known at that time for practising rational-emotive therapy, and in those days I was far less flexible in its practice than I think I am now.

One evening I received a call from a man who said he had been referred to me for what he called 'RT therapy'. Before rational-emotive therapy was known as 'RET' it was called 'rational therapy', or 'RT' for short. I remember thinking it was a bit odd for someone to call RET by its older abbreviation 'RT'; however, I did not pursue it over the phone, and we proceeded to make an appointment for an assessment session.

After telling me about his various problems, the man asked how I thought I could help him. I responded with a brief overview of RET, how his problems could be traced to a number of faulty beliefs and attitudes, and how we would work together to help him to identify, challenge, and change these beliefs. He listened patiently, but after I had finished he shook his head and said he hadn't heard such a load of intellectualised rubbish in a long time.

Apparently, the person who effected the referral mistook RET for Reichian therapy (RT), a body-orientated approach to therapy which is based on the idea that people's problems are related to energy blockages that are located in various parts of the body, and which require body-orientated interventions such as deep massage. These interventions will, according to the theory, help to free these blockages so that the person's psychic energy can be restored. As you may appreciate, this is a far cry from the theory and practice of RET, so instead of trying to disabuse the man of his ideas of what caused his problems and what he considered he needed to resolve them, I effected a further referral to a local therapist who I knew used Reichian techniques. I heard later that my referral yielded very positive results for the client. This experience led me to begin to question the unquestionable: perhaps I couldn't help everyone.

This tentatively held conclusion was strengthened as my name began to become more widely known in the counselling community. However, as this happened, increasingly I received calls from prospective female clients who either thought my name was 'Wendy' Dryden, or that Windy was a woman's name. A typical conversation would go like this:

> *Woman:* Can I speak to Windy Dryden please?
> *Me:* Speaking. How can I help you?
> *Woman:* No, I'm sorry, you misheard me. I asked for Windy Dryden. She's a female counsellor.
> *Me:* My name is Windy Dryden. I'm often mistaken for a woman because of my first name.
> *Woman:* I'm sorry to trouble you, but I'm looking for a woman counsellor. 'Bye.

I have had this kind of conversation many times now. In fact, I have gained much first-hand experience of numerous women not wanting to see me for counselling because I am a man.

These and similar experiences have led me to conclude that I may well not be the best person to help a client. I am much more comfortable with this idea now, at a time when I am confident in my ability as a counsellor, than I was earlier in my career when I was more uncertain of this ability, and when I had more to prove to myself.

The consequences of realising that I may not be the best person to help is that I now refer prospective clients to other counsellors a lot more than I used to. As Arnold Lazarus has put it (Dryden, 1991), one of our tasks in counselling is to know our own limitations and other counsellors' strengths. By all means we should work to minimise our limitations, but since we will always have our fallibilities as practitioners, it behoves us to refer clients to others who are better placed to help. I can now do this with satisfaction, whereas earlier in my career, if I did it at all, it was with a sense of failure.

'You didn't ask me!'

One of the most painful lessons I have had to learn as a counsellor is that sometimes I just don't seem to learn — that I seem to make the same mistakes over and over again. When I first discovered this, I thought it applied just to me, since I hadn't read about it in the counselling literature. However, the more I supervised counsellors' tapes, which gave me access to what counsellors actually did in their sessions, as opposed to what they said they did, the more I realised, with relief, that it applied to other people as well.

A vivid example of this stands out in my mind. As I have mentioned, in 1981 I spent a six-month sabbatical at the Center for Cognitive Therapy in Philadelphia. One of the clients I saw there was a forty-two-year-old housewife who was severely depressed. She had had psychoanalytic psychotherapy without any appreciable benefit, and was referred to the Center as it had a growing reputation for the treatment of depression.

The client, whom I will call Phyllis, responded very well to cognitive therapy, and in five months or so her score on the Beck Depression Inventory went from being in the severely depressed range to being in the non-depressed range. At the end of the therapy the client seemed happy with the outcome of our work together. I was also happy, and so was my supervisor. Now, one of the features of the therapy that accounted for its success, or so I thought, was the quality of our relationship. Phyllis and I seemed to get on rather well, and she had a good sense of humour, which I capitalised on during the therapy. At times this humour seemed to be what I called 'overly giggly', but I attributed this to the exuberance of Phyllis's personality. How wrong I was!

A year later I returned to the Center for a visit, and was encouraged to schedule a follow-up session with all the clients I had seen a year previously. Among these was Phyllis. When I met her, she seemed altogether more serious than when I had known her. She had maintained the gains she had made in therapy with me with respect to her depression, but mentioned, almost casually, that in the past year she had had treatment for 'my long-standing alcohol abuse problem'. 'What long-standing alcohol abuse problem? You didn't tell me you had an alcohol problem', I whined pitifully, or so it seems now, many years later. 'Well,' she replied with more than a hint of irony in her voice, *'you didn't ask me!'* As you can imagine, I didn't feel too good about this, which of course is an understatement. I felt wretched. My initial reaction was to write to the University of Aston, which employed me at that time, and tender my resignation. How could I possibly train counsellors if I could make such ridiculous blunder? However, common sense prevailed, and instead I resolved to ask all my subsequent clients about their drinking and drug intake, which I did, or so I thought I did until the episode with Emily.

Emily was an artist who, among other concerns, spoke of feelings of emptiness. I had been working with her for about two years, during which she had begun to extricate herself from being trapped in her vocation by enrolling for a university course. She also had made reasonable progress in overcoming long-standing social and performance-related anxieties. However, we had arrived at an impasse, and Emily came to sessions with increasing anxiety, for which she offered no clear explanation. I realised something was amiss, but couldn't put my finger on what this was. Soon after, Emily came to a session in a state of extreme anxiety and handed me a letter to read. In it, Emily admitted that she had a long-standing drink problem, consuming regularly a bottle of wine a day. Dumbfounded, I again blurted out the question, 'Why haven't you told me before?' I saw my whole counselling life flash before my eyes as I processed her reply, which was, as you may have guessed, *'You didn't ask me!'*

I have several other examples where I mistakenly thought I had learned a lesson from counselling once and for all, but this is the most striking. Of course, there are several important questions to ask about my seeming lapse and, believe me, I have asked them both inside and outside supervision. The point I want to stress here is that as counsellors we don't learn something once and for all. We are human and subject to all the fallibilities this status endows. In counselling this may well mean we have our blind spots. For my own part, while I will of course resolve once again to ask all my clients about their drinking habits, I will be less horrified — but not less chastened — when some future client responds to my enquiry about their failures to disclose a secret drinking problem with the statement, *'You didn't ask me!'*

Conclusion

On re-reading these five hard-earned lessons, two major themes stand out: the importance of variety in counselling, and the inevitability of counsellor fallibility. The variety theme occurs in the first four lessons. In the first, I learned that I thrive on variety in my working life and that I would wilt, to some degree, if I ever had to work full-time as a counsellor for more than a short period of time. In lessons two and three, I learned that clients need a variety of responses from their counsellors in both the bond and task domains of the working counselling alliance. In lesson four I learned that if an individual counsellor has sufficient flexibility and authenticity to provide such varied responses to a broad range of clients, all is well and good; if not, then he or she should unashamedly refer them on to other practitioners who are more suitable.

The second theme concerns the fact that, being human, all counsellors have limitations. This theme is present in all five lessons. It appears in the first lesson in the guise of my own personal limitations concerning the composition of my working life. Apparently, I function much better in a work setting where there is scope for diversity. If I am to retain my enthusiasm for the field of counselling and to avoid burnout, then one way I can do this is to avoid a restricting range of work tasks. For some, working as a full-time practitioner provides sufficient variety, but not for me.

In lessons two and three I discussed the theme of counsellor limitations more implicitly. If different clients require a different kind of bond with their counsellors, even the most interpersonally flexible of counsellors will not be able to help everyone. Be as flexible as you authentically can, but know your interpersonal limitations is the message of lesson two, while a similar message, but with respect to the use of counselling tasks, is to be found in lesson three. The obvious conclusion in the light of the limitations of individual counsellors occurs in lesson four: don't hesitate to refer to other counsellors when you come up against your own limitations. Having limitations is inevitable, so you don't need to be ashamed of them is a message I would like to convey to beginning counsellors.

Although it is crucial for all counsellors to minimise their errors, the fifth and final lesson demonstrates that we may well come up against blind spots that defy mastery. It might be nice if we could eliminate all our blind spots, but maybe the consequent loss of our humanity would make us less helpful to our human clients. Perhaps that is the most helpful lesson of all.

References

Bordin, E. S. (1979) The generalizability of the psychoanalytic concept of the working alliance. *Psychotherapy: Theory. Research and Practice, 16,* 252–60.

Dryden, W. (1984) Rational-emotive therapy and cognitive therapy: a critical comparison. In M. A. Reda and M. J. Mahoney (eds.), *Cognitive Psychotherapies: Recent Developments in Theory, Research and Practice.* Cambridge, Massachusetts: Ballinger.

Dryden, W. (1991) *A Dialogue with Arnold Lazarus: 'It Depends'.* Milton Keynes: Open University Press.

Lazarus, A. A. (1981) *The Practice of Multimodal Therapy.* New York: McGraw-Hill.

5

what I wished I'd learned during counsellor training, what I'm glad I did and didn't learn and what I'm sorry that I did

What I want to do in this chapter is to take a look at my main professional training as a counsellor and consider four things: (a) what I wished I had learned from this training experience; (b) what I am glad I did learn; (c) what I am glad I did not learn and (d) what I'm sorry that I learnt. In reviewing my training, I came to the disconcerting conclusion that I am something of an old timer in the counselling field. I don't 'feel' like an old timer; in fact, I 'feel' like a spring chicken. However, reluctantly, I have to admit that I am an old timer; after all I first trained professionally as a counsellor in 1974.

While I will confine myself to my initial extended training experience, I will refer to my other training experiences which I will briefly outline for you in case you are interested. I began my professional training in counselling with a one-year, full-time course at Aston University, which was basically a person-centred counselling course. After this, I did a two-year, part-time course in psychodynamic psychotherapy at the training section of Uffculme Clinic which later became the West Midlands Institute for Psychotherapy. This was basically an introductory course which I did not complete because during the second year of this course I decided to pursue training in Rational Emotive Behaviour Therapy which I did part-time in New York from 1977 until 1979. In 1978, I also took a two-year, part-time MSc course in Psychotherapy at Warwick University. This was a broad, eclectic course which complemented the REBT training that I was pursuing at the same time. Finally, in 1981, I took a sabbatical from my university job and spent six months full-time at the Center for Cognitive Therapy with Aaron Beck in Philadelphia, learning cognitive therapy.

When I initially trained in 1974, training opportunities outside Marriage Guidance were few and far between and they were largely confined to the field of counselling in education. The main courses available at that time were all one-year full-time in nature and were based in the universities of Reading, Keele, Swansea and Aston. The first three named courses were focused on school counselling and were largely open to serving teachers who attended the courses on sabbatical. Yes that's right, serving teachers were given a year off on full pay and were seconded to train as school counsellors. Happy days! The other course at the University of Aston in Birmingham was focused on counselling in higher educational settings and attracted a generous number of Department of Education and Science (DES) State Bursaries. This meant that the State paid recipients' fees and gave them, in addition, an ample living grant. I was the fortunate recipient of one of these State Bursaries when I took up a place on Aston's one- year Diploma in Counselling in Educational Settings course in the 1974/5 academic year. Prior to this I had done the first year of the South West London College counselling course which later became a self-directed training course (Charleton, 1996), had been a Nightline worker, a Samaritan and worked part-time in the Student Counselling Service at University College, London where Pat Milner was Student Counsellor. So I had a good introductory grounding in the theory and skills of counselling before I began at Aston.

Two of the strengths of the Aston course were its generous staff–student ratio and the calibre of its trainers. On my course there were seventeen full-time students and the course was staffed by two full-time tutors. The course tutor was Richard Nelson-Jones, who will no doubt be known to you from his books on counselling, and the other tutor was Don Biggs, a Fulbright Fellow. Fulbright Fellows were leading counsellor trainers from North America, seconded to Aston for the purpose of helping Richard Nelson-Jones to provide a professional counsellor training for student counsellors. Previous 'Fulbrights' were C. H. Patterson and Stanley Strong, both internationally known counselling psychologists. So, I was fortunate to be trained by well-respected, experienced trainers who worked under a student–staff ratio of 8.5 to 1. I think that you would be hard placed to find a course in Britain today with these two characteristics.

Another feature of the training course at Aston at that time was that it was full-time. Then, full-time meant full-time. We had one afternoon off for private study, but for the rest of the time we were fully occupied either at college or at our placements which were arranged for us by the course tutor. Nowadays, a full-time counselling course can literally mean full-time, but it more often means far less. Indeed, it is possible today to do a one-year, full-time counselling course by attending college for two days only. In addition, either you have to be in practice already or you have to organise your own placement. So we got a very good deal at Aston with respect to the amount of training we received over a very full academic year and with respect to the assistance we were given with our placements.

Another good aspect of the Aston training course was that it ran intensive skills-based workshops in the first term where we focused in small groups on basic counselling skills. In these groups, we repeatedly made videos of our peer counselling sessions which were then studied in detail with the purpose of enhancing skill development. What was valuable here was that each individual student made an extended video of his or her counselling skills and had plenty of time to learn how to improve these skills. At the end of the first term, we had to pass a number of 'readiness to see clients' assessments which comprised a video of our counselling skills and an exam which assessed core knowledge such as being able to identify signs that clients are severely disturbed; being able to articulate the indications and contraindications of counselling and other forms of helping and demonstrating a working knowledge of relevant information about the major psychotropic drugs. These assessments were very useful in helping us to focus our attention on what we had to learn and on understanding why this knowledge and these skills were fundamental to seeing clients.

I mentioned at the outset that the course at Aston at that time was person-centred in orientation. This meant that I did not learn, for example, the importance of taking a history from my clients. I later learned that this was important because it helped me to gain an overall understanding of my clients by discovering amongst other things: (a) the origin and development of my clients' problems, (b) their family background and (c) their use of alcohol and drugs. I recently wrote an article outlining my approach to a growing area known as case formulation, which involves developing an overall understanding of clients in the context of their problems and where hypotheses concerning the mechanisms underpinning clients' problems are put forward with the purpose of giving a direction and coherence to counselling, thus aiding treatment planning (Dryden, 1999). This would never have been taught on the Aston course where, in keeping with the views of Rogers (1951), assessment in counselling was not considered to have a valid role. This had the effect of accentuating the confusion many of us experienced when we began to see clients because we didn't have an overall understanding of the clients whom we were seeing. As most of you know, assessment is scorned in person-centred counselling because it is seen as emanating from the frame of reference of the counsellor, and the prime directive (if I can borrow a phrase from Star Trek) for person-centred counsellors is to remain, whenever possible, within the frame of reference of the client. I wish I had learned then that working with clients from *both* an external *and* an internal frame of reference is acceptable and therapeutic and it is more a question of when to work within a particular frame of reference than of which frame of reference to work within.

We also did not learn at Aston how to plan counselling over its course. Although Rogers (1951) did outline the stages that clients tend to go through in person-centred counselling, he argued that this occurs as a matter of course if clients experience their counsellors as empathic, warm and genuine. If provision of the core conditions is necessary and sufficient for constructive client change to occur (assuming that these conditions are experienced by the client), then there is no need for treatment planning, a concept which is predicated on the notion that counsellors need to intervene in different ways with different clients. Fortunately, I later learned about this concept on the MSc in Psychotherapy course at Warwick.

Having said all of this. I am glad that we were trained in a model that was systematic even if it does have, in my view, serious limitations.

This meant that we could immerse ourselves in the philosophical ideas underpinning the approach, study its model of the person, explore in full its view of psychological health and disturbance, evaluate its view of the acquisition and perpetuation of psychological disturbance and of psychological change and evaluate the influence of all of these ideas on its suggestions for counselling practice. Some of you will recognise some of these points as chapter headings from my textbook *Handbook of Individual Therapy* (Dryden, 1996). I fully acknowledge the influence that the Aston counselling course has had on this book and this, I believe, shows one of the benefits of studying an approach in depth and in a structured way.

There is at present a debate in the literature about the value of studying a core model in professional counsellor training. Its proponents, like myself, argue that doing so enables the trainee to study something in depth and be offered a useful framework for practice even if this framework is limited (Dryden, Horton & Mearns, 1995). In other words, it gives trainees a roadmap for practice. Now, of course, there is the danger that trainees then think that this is the only way to practise, but this attitude can be elicited and dealt with on the course, particularly if staff members have a flexible attitude towards the core model. Antagonists (e.g. Feltham, 1997) argue that since no one model is more effective than any other it is premature to teach a core model and a more flexible, eclectic approach to counsellor training should be implemented. This makes intuitive sense, but there are real inherent dangers to this approach. First, for such an approach to work, the training has to be delivered by people who are highly experienced in the field and have developed a mature eclectic or integrative approach over many years and can teach this clearly and coherently. The danger, then, lies in training being provided by inexperienced people whose eclecticism or integration has been introjected, rather than developed over time and who are unable to bring the disparate elements of practice into a coherent whole. What is problematic here is the lack of a coherent and systematic approach to training.

In this context, let me say a few words about my concerns about the present approach adopted within counselling psychology training in Britain. In order for a counselling psychology course to be accredited by the British Psychological Society, its trainees have to learn at least two models of counselling as well as take a number of other theory and research modules not centrally related to these two counselling approaches. Such courses are usually two-years part-time. Now, at present I run a two-year, part-time MSc course in Rational Emotive Behaviour Therapy. I find that this duration is just sufficient to enable me to train my students to competence in that one approach to counselling. So, I really wonder what level of competence counselling psychology trainees can attain in learning two counselling approaches at the same time as following other modules. Perhaps it is not the intention of counselling psychology courses to train competent counsellors. If not, who are they trying to train? If so, I wonder how they achieve this because I know that I couldn't. So, in conclusion, I'm glad that I learned from my original course the value of systematic training in a core theoretical model especially when the limits and weaknesses of that model are fully explored.

A counselling course is very much influenced by its trainers and ours was no exception. During the year that I was at Aston, there were initial signs that Richard Nelson-Jones was beginning to move away from person-centred counselling and develop his own integrative approach to counselling which he expanded on in much greater detail later (Nelson-Jones, 1984). However, at that time he was still largely influenced by Rogers' ideas and the Aston course was still at heart a person-centred one. This is not to say that we did not study other approaches to counselling. Far from it. Richard Nelson-Jones gave a very good counselling theories course and provided extremely useful handouts which were later expanded into his book, *The Theory and Practice of Counselling Psychology* (Nelson-Jones, 1982). We also had a term's course on behavioural counselling which was run by a university lecturer from Birmingham University who was a behaviourally-oriented clinical psychologist. However, there was always the sense that behavioural methods were best used with clients who had specific fears and phobias or study and social skills difficulties while person-centred counselling should be used with everybody else.

What I did not learn on the course and wished that I had was the limits of person-centred counselling and the importance of a 'horses for courses' approach i.e. which therapeutic methods are best used with which clients experiencing which problems. To be fair to the course, such issues were not actively discussed in the counselling literature in 1974/5 to the extent that they are today. This issue became salient for me because I had a number of clients who wanted more from me than the empathy, warmth and genuineness I was offering them. Because I thought at the time that person-centred counselling was the be all and end all of the counselling world, I concluded that the fault must lie within me rather than in the interaction between person-centred counselling and the clients themselves. No, because I was sure that person-centred counselling did not have limitations, I concluded that the reason that some of my clients wanted more was that I was deficient in offering the core conditions and if only I could be more empathic, warm and genuine then these clients would respond better to my counselling. Now, while I think that there may have been a grain of truth to this analysis, I am more persuaded by the argument that clients respond differently to different therapeutic methods. It took me quite a while to recover from this self-inflicted blow to my confidence, but I am sure that this wouldn't have happened to such a degree if, as I said before, the course was more systematic in dealing with the strengths and weaknesses of person-centred counselling. I think that it is so important that any course be rigorous in looking critically at the core model on which the course is based and to help trainees understand that if clients don't improve it may not be due to the counsellor or to the client, but to the fact that the client may be better suited to a different therapeutic approach.

While there are plenty of casebooks in the field of counselling and psychotherapy where brief descriptive information is provided of 'cases' from beginning to end, there is a dearth of material where verbatim transcripts are made available which show in detail the course of therapy. This mirrors many training courses where trainers may discuss their work with different clients, but do not demonstrate this work by allowing their trainees to watch videos or listen to audiotapes of counselling sessions that they have conducted with clients over the entire therapeutic process. This was the case with the course at Aston. Not only did the trainers not demonstrate their work over time with clients, they also did not show us how they worked with clients at all. This meant that we had very little practical idea of how to work with clients over time. We read articles on the therapeutic process and we received supervision on our work with clients from the beginning to the end of the therapeutic process, but we were not shown how to practise counselling over time. This was a significant gap in our education and something that I wished we had covered in that year.

Related to this, since we were not exposed to the work that our Aston trainers actually did with their clients, we were not exposed to helpful role models for effective counselling. Although we did view various videotapes of leading counselling figures working directly with clients in demonstration sessions (notably Rogers, Ellis and Perls working with the now infamous Gloria), this was no substitute for viewing on videotape or hearing on audiotape the work of people whom we could then question in depth about why they responded in the way that they did. Fortunately, after Aston I was able to observe master therapists working directly with clients and to discuss with them at length their interventions and why they made them. Thus, in 1978, as part of my REBT training, I served as associate therapist in Albert Ellis's four evening therapy groups during the month of August when his regular associate therapists were on vacation. This was done with the permission of the group members. I found this invaluable not only because it gave me the opportunity to observe closely the originator of REBT working with a number of very different patients, but because it also allowed me to question him later on the nature and purpose of his interventions. I cannot think of a better way of learning to be a group therapist.

Then, a number of years later, I spent two full weeks sitting in with Arnold Lazarus as he conducted his individual sessions. For those of you who do not know Arnold Lazarus he is best known for his pioneering work on technical eclecticism and multimodal therapy. Again this was done with the expressed permission of his clients. After each day's work I would question Lazarus about the work he was doing with each of his different clients which was more valuable to me than reading two years' worth of counselling and psychotherapy books.

In addition, since I was permitted to intervene in both Ellis's groups and Lazarus's individual sessions, they also gave me valuable feedback on my own interventions. This apprenticeship model of counsellor training is perhaps the best form of training that has been devised and is one that is least used. Of course, it does not easily lend itself to training in psychodynamic counselling and person-centred counselling and this perhaps explains why it is so rare. But I would rate these brief episodes of working closely with two master therapists as easily the most valuable form of training that I have received.

Let me now consider what I am glad that I didn't learn in my time as a trainee on the Aston counselling course. First, I did not learn that it was important to study human growth and development in depth in order to practise counselling effectively. While I am not against trainee counsellors learning about human development, it seems to me that on a busy curriculum the in-depth study of this subject has a fairly low priority when practising counselling effectively is the criterion for inclusion and exclusion of a topic. If I practised psychodynamic counselling I would probably have a different view, but in the practice of cognitive-behaviour therapy in general and Rational Emotive Behaviour Therapy in particular this subject is dispensable.

Second, I did not learn that case discussion is a central part of counsellor training. Rather, I learned that it was important to make and present for supervision audiotapes of my counselling sessions so that I could reflect on what actually happened between my client and myself rather than on my account of what happened. Again, I am not saying that discussion of cases has no useful place in counsellor training. Indeed, I think that it is important when it comes to monitoring case formulation and treatment planning issues. But case discussion to the exclusion of the study of audiotapes of counselling sessions is not very helpful and I'm glad that I did not learn at Aston that it was.

Third, I am glad that I did not learn at Aston that personal therapy is an essential part of counsellor training. I am not against trainees seeking personal therapy if they do so for personal reasons or if they think that it will help them deal with the stresses of counselling practice. But I am not in favour of such personal therapy being a mandatory part of counsellor training. While there is much evidence that trained therapists think that personal therapy was an important part of their training and even that such therapy made them more effective practitioners, there is little evidence that receiving personal therapy actually makes therapists more effective with their clients. As I have discussed elsewhere, it may well be that the reason why personal therapy does not increase one's effectiveness as a counsellor is that it does not focus on one's work as a counsellor and one's feelings towards one's clients. Rather, it tends to be unrestricted and trainees can talk about anything that they wish to discuss with their personal therapists. I have in mind a form of personal therapy which I have called 'client-centred' personal therapy (Dryden, 1994) where discussion is focused on client work and the feelings that one experiences in working with clients as a foundation for exploration. I would like to see a research study conducted into the comparative impact of traditional personal therapy and 'client-centred' personal therapy on counsellor effectiveness. Only then will we be able to see the true value of personal therapy in the wider context of counsellor training.

Let me now consider briefly the main thing that I learned during my counsellor training at Aston that I wished that I hadn't learned. This concerned the role that the personal development group has in counsellor training. Even though the personal development group I attended during that year at Aston was not a growthful experience for me and as far as I can tell for any of my fellow trainees, we were frequently assured that this was a very important part of our experience as a counsellor trainee. And I am afraid that I accepted this logic unquestioningly. However, two subsequent types of experience have led me to revise my opinion significantly on this point. The first set of experiences relates to personal development groups that I attended as part of my subsequent training and the second relates to my trainees' experiences of the personal development groups that they attended as part of their training on the courses that I organised.

Let me consider first my further experiences of being a member of personal development groups. I attended two groups as part of my psychodynamic training. The first was called a transference group and the second a personal development group although they were to my untutored eyes completely indistinguishable. Once again, I gained little from these groups and so according to their own report did my fellow group members. It was generally thought that seeing one another in other parts of the course served as an inhibiting factor when it came to what we were prepared to disclose about ourselves to one another. Then on the Masters course in Psychotherapy at Warwick I attended a two-year personal development group with similar results and with similar concerns expressed by group members. I have thus attended four personal development groups over a five-year period and cannot say that any of them were personally beneficial experiences. None was harmful, to be sure, but none was particularly helpful and none improved my effectiveness as a counsellor.

When I became a counsellor trainer, I included personal development groups on the curriculum, not because I believed that they are an essential part of counsellor training, but because, in general, the field does. This despite the fact that such groups are routinely given low ratings by students with respect to how useful they are to improving one's competence as a counsellor. If, given the proper resources, I can reorganise my present MSc in Rational Emotive Behaviour Therapy so that it is eligible for BACP and UKCP accreditation, I will still include these groups on the curriculum. But I will do so because they are required for such accreditation and not because I think that they are terribly useful.

If attending a personal development group is to be a mandatory part of counsellor training then it is my view that ideally trainees should join such a group where no other member of their training cohort is present so that they can disclose themselves in the knowledge that they will not meet other group members in other settings. Even then, I am not persuaded of the value of such groups in the counsellor training process, but at least it would meet the oft-repeated criticism by trainees that personal development groups comprising course members inhibit full participation and relevant personal disclosure.

Let me conclude my discussion by considering briefly the impact that practical and contextual constraints have on counsellor training and the compromises that have to be made as a result. In many ways, the Aston counselling course was very well funded. In 1974/5 the phrase 'educational cuts' had not yet been heard and this was reflected in the very generous staff–student ratio that existed then which, as I have already stated, enabled counselling skills workshops to be run giving each individual ample time to practise, to be fully observed and to be given proper feedback. While this funding was generous when compared to that received by counselling courses today, even then the course tutor complained that the Aston course was not funded as a 'clinical' course which, if it had been, would have made the staff–student ratio even more generous. In higher education today, funding on many professional level counselling courses does not often permit staff–student ratios low enough for each student to get sufficient individual attention for skill acquisition and refinement. This applies to the Masters course that I run, so reluctantly I have had to compromise with my own training values.

Thus, the skills training workshops that I run have a staff–student ratio of 1:16 when at Aston it was 1:8.5, almost half what it is on my course. This has meant that I do not have the time to give each of my trainees sufficient attention as they struggle to learn complex practical skills. My dilemma is that if I do reorganise the course to give students the individual attention that they warrant, I could not offer a Masters course since it would not meet university criteria for a Masters course. So, I compromise and struggle as best I can with the resources at my disposal. Sometimes I think that given present funding levels institutions of higher education are not ideal environments for running counsellor training courses. But, were I to run my ideal REBT training course in a private institution, then the fees would be so high that it would exclude all but the most well-off trainee.

Perhaps you would have liked me to have ended on a more optimistic note. I certainly would have liked to have done so. At times like these I look back with envy at my time at Aston; but counselling is about dealing with reality and not about living nostalgically in the past. So if counsellor trainers like myself are to continue to train counsellors, then we have to work within the means at our disposal. I still have my dreams though and one day I hope to run a training course according to my ideals.

References

Charleton, M. (1996). *Self-directed Learning in Counsellor Training*. London: Cassell.

Dryden. W. (1994). Possible future trends in counselling and counsellor training: A personal view. *Counselling: The Journal of BAC*. 5(3), 194–7.

Dryden, W. (ed.) (1996). *Handbook of Individual Therapy*. London: Sage.

Dryden. W. (1999). *Rational Emotive Behaviour Therapy: A Personal Approach*. Oxford: Winslow Press.

Dryden, W., Horton, I. & Mearns, D. (1995). *Issues in Professional Counsellor Training*. London: Cassell.

Feltham, C. (1997). Challenging the core theoretical model. *Counselling: The Journal BAC*, 8(2), 121–5.

Nelson-Jones, R. (1982). *The Theory and Practice of Counselling Psychology*. London: Cassell.

Nelson-Jones, R. (1984). *Personal Responsibility Counselling and Therapy: An Integrative Approach*. London: Harper & Row.

Rogers. C.R. (1951). *Client-Centered Therapy*. London: Constable.

A version of this chapter was given to the Wimbledon Guild on 18 April 1998.

6

religion, spirituality and human worth

Personal perspectives
Religious label
I should say at the outset of this chapter that religion plays a peripheral, almost non-existent role in my life and has done ever since I was barmitzvahed. However, my parents are Jewish, I was brought up as a Jew and my wife is Jewish and as such Jewish issues are present in my life. To put it simply, I regard myself as Jewish by culture, but not by religion. If pressed to put a label on my religious orientation I would say that I was a probabilistic atheist and an environmental humanist. By a probabilistic atheist I mean that I very much doubt the existence of a deity, but am not prepared to state this as an absolute fact. By an environmental humanist I mean that I believe that while human affairs and the collective physical and psychological well-being of humans are paramount on this planet, the well-being of other organisms and the environment are to be carefully considered.

Personal position on spirituality
I have always struggled to understand what people mean by the term 'spirituality'. I have always recoiled from it for a number of reasons. First, for me it conjures up matters to do with the 'spirit' and I find it difficult to hear this term without hearing the word 'holy' in front of it. Also, rightly or wrongly, I associate the term 'spiritual' with the term 'transpersonal' and indeed for some transpersonal experiences and one's relationship with whatever one considers to be the 'Ultimate' are defining characteristics of being spiritual. If these are essential characteristics of spirituality, I am not spiritual. However, let me outline part of a definition of spirituality that I can live with, if certain modifications are made to it. Kelly (1995) as has said that:

> the identifiable values of spirituality include confidence in the meaning and purpose of life, a sense of mission in life and of the sacredness of life, a balanced appreciation of material values, an altruistic attitude towards others, a vision for the betterment of the world and a seriousness of the tragic side of life (p.4).

Using this as a starting point, I would say that I was spiritual in the sense that there are several major meanings and purposes to my life and that one central one is doing what I can personally and professionally to improve the mental health of my fellow humans. I regard life as something to be cherished but not as sacred and I am aware of the tragic, comic, ironic and romantic sides of life. I, thus, see balance in life and certainly strive to marry my material and non-material interests with those of others and those of the environment.

Religious and spiritual experiences
My *religious* experiences have in the main been negative. I was made to go to Hebrew classes three nights a week and every Sunday morning until I turned 13. I hated virtually every minute of it. If I had a different psychological perspective I would say that I was religiously abused in that I was forced to go to these classes against my will. My own viewpoint is that I was forced to endure what I saw as hours of meaningless religious study, none of which I took seriously. As soon as I had my barmitzvah, that was that. I stopped going to synagogue and only got married in one because my wife, Louise, would not have married me in any other setting.

When I think of an experience that might be regarded as *spiritual* in nature I think of one that others might not regard in this category. I was sitting in the kitchen in my boyhood home in 1965 when I heard on the radio the sound of a shotgun followed by a drum roll and a raunchy, soulful saxophone which hit me like a bolt out of the blue. I was transfixed, felt weak at the knees and tingled all over. It was a record called 'Shotgun' by Jr. Walker and the All Stars, which I rushed out there and then to buy. All I can say is that for some reason I deeply resonated to the sounds that I heard that day in a way that defied and still defies understanding. We weren't a musical family and there was no family tradition of listening to blues or soul music that may have prepared the ground for my response. If I had a soul (which I very much doubt), I would say that it was touched that day by Jr. Walker.

The aftermath of this experience is interesting. I was moved by it to take up the saxophone, for which sadly I had no talent. However, I did acquire the nickname 'Windy', from these days and when I changed my surname in the late 1960s I changed my first name too. I went from being David Denbin to Windy Dryden. So that experience 37 years ago has had an enduring impact on me. Not only do I still resonate to the music of Jr. Walker (who sadly passed away in 1993), it led to my name change.

Professional issues
Impact of personal religious and spiritual background on REBT practice
I am wary of speculating on the impact that the above experiences may have had on my REBT practice with clients since these experiences may have been influenced by factors that may have more of an impact

than the experiences themselves. Having said this, I would say that such experiences and their underlying determinants have influenced my clinical work as follows.

i.   My negative experiences with Jewish religious education has led me to be particularly alert to situations where clients have accepted the religious and non-religious viewpoints of others without question. This is a delicate area. As an REBT therapist I value independent thinking and would want to facilitate such thinking in clients. Yet I am very aware of the dangers imposing independent thinking on clients, particularly in areas where they have not indicated having a problem. I have found that the way out of this dilemma is to bring such instances of uncritical internalisation of others' viewpoints to the attention of my clients only where it is relevant to their emotional problems and to show them that they have a choice of what to believe. For example, I have seen several orthodox Jewish clients who have had an emotional problem about masturbation and whose uncritical acceptance of the religious viewpoint that the spilling of one's own seed is a sin has been centrally involved in their problem. I have shown such clients that: (a) there are other ways of viewing masturbation; (b) there are implications of each viewpoint; (c) they can choose what to believe; and (d) I will work to help them, whatever they choose. If a client chooses to continue to see masturbation as a sin, I will help him to refrain from this activity and highlight for change low frustration tolerance beliefs that lead him into temptation. On the other hand, if he decides, after reflection, to view masturbation as a natural male activity and not inherently sinful, I will help him to identify and overcome his guilt-related beliefs about going against his religious teachings. My position is to respect the client's wishes and to work within his (in this case) chosen frame of reference.

ii. My Jr. Walker 'spiritual' experience has taught me several things. First, people can deeply resonate to a variety of things and such deep resonance may not be explainable. Second, I respect and take seriously clients' spiritual experiences, whatever they are, even if I don't understand them or if they seem silly from my frame of reference. The experience is more important than the content, and therapist respect for the experience is more important than therapist understanding of the content. Third, looking for historical determinants of 'spiritual' and non-spiritual experiences may not be that helpful from a clinical perspective. This, of course, is echoed in REBT's phenomenological view of client experience.

Human worth and the understanding of evil
I am an REBT therapist for a number of reasons (Dryden, 2001), but none more so than for its position on human worth. This very much resonates with my humanist leanings. In fact, REBT has two perspectives on human worth. The most radical is that humans are neither worthwhile nor worthless since they are too complex to be globally rated. Rather, they are human and as such they can either accept themselves or reject themselves. If they accept themselves and others as humans who are all equal in humanity to one another, this will promote the psychological health and well-being of all humans. This position does not prevent humans from rating aspects of themselves (and others) and thus from dealing with the negative aspects of themselves (and others) and capitalising on the positive aspects of themselves (and others). The second, less radical, perspective is that all humans are worthwhile because they are alive, all humans are equal in worth to one another because of their humanity and their aliveness, but they are unequal in rateable aspects of themselves. Again, this position is deemed to promote the psychological health and well-being of humans. See Ellis (1972) for a full discussion of both perspectives.

My own view is that Osama bin Laden, assuming that he was the architect of the September 11 atrocities, is not an evil person, but he is guilty of promoting evil acts that cannot be justified from a humanist perspective (and from many other perspectives too). Viewing people such as bin Laden as evil is easy to do and not doing so may wrongly be seen as failing to condemn what they did. However, viewing them as evil may have several negative consequences:

i.   It may prevent us from seeking to understand the thinking behind their actions, understanding which may help us to take action designed to make such atrocities less likely from happening again in the future.

ii.   It may lead us to view others who act in ways that go against our valued interests as evil.

iii.   Viewing people such as bin Laden as evil makes it less likely that we will negotiate with them before they commit such atrocities.

iv.   Public declarations that people such as bin Laden are evil may harden the attitude of their followers and increase the possibility that these followers will commit further atrocities in the future.

v. Viewing people as evil will make it more likely that we will commit atrocities against them which we will then justify as appropriate responses to their atrocities.

vi. Treating people as evil and worthless may lead them to regard themselves as worthless and evil and increase the chances that they will act in ways that are consistent with these self-views.

I am not saying that an attitude of other acceptance is without negative consequences, but in accordance with REBT theory I would say that such consequences would be fewer and less deleterious to the person holding the attitude, to the object of the attitude and to the world in general.

Issues of self-depreciation and other depreciation occur in the clinic very frequently, although rarely about people such as Osama bin Laden. The clinical implications of what I have said in this chapter in addressing such issues are as follows:

i. I strive to help clients see the link between self-depreciation (SD) /other depreciation (OD) and the emotional and behavioural problems that they wish to change.

ii. I outline and explain the concepts of unconditional self-acceptance (USA) and unconditional other acceptance (UOA) and help clients to see what difference holding such attitudes would make to their emotions and behaviours.

iii. I outline common doubts, reservations and objections to USA and UOA and engage clients in an open discussion about these and others that they may personally hold about these concepts.

iv. I encourage clients to do a thorough cost–benefit analysis about the short-term and long-term advantages and disadvantages to self and others of holding SD vs. USA beliefs and OD vs. UOA beliefs and engage them in an open discussion of these, correcting misconceptions as they are disclosed.

v. I encourage clients to see that they and only they can choose which attitudes to hold, and while I am biased in favour of USA and UOA they should make their own minds up about which attitudes they wish to hold.

vi. If clients choose to hold the attitudes of USA and UOA, I encourage them to make a commitment to work towards holding these beliefs and outline the process that this typically involves: it is a lengthy process which often involves thinking and acting in unnatural ways until they become natural, and like self-actualisation it is a process, not an end state to be achieved once and for all.

Conclusion

In this chapter I have outlined my views on religion, spirituality and evil and discussed some of the clinical implications of these views in my REBT practice. I am surprised about the central role that I have given to encouraging people to think for themselves. On reflection, the negative impact of forced religious instruction was greater than I had thought and helps to explain why I would rather clients thinkingly reject REBT concepts than unthinkingly accept them. I could even say that such a revelation was spiritual in nature!

References

Dryden, W. (2001). How rational am I?: Self-help using rational emotive behaviour therapy. In E. Spinelli & S. Marshall (eds.), *Embodied Theories* (pp. 28–42). London: Continuum.

Ellis, A. (1972). *Psychotherapy and the Value of a Human Being.* New York: Albert Ellis Institute for REBT.

Kelly, E. W. Jr. (1995). *Spirituality and Religion in Counselling and Psychotherapy: Diversity in Theory and Practice.* Lanham, MD: University Press of America.

7

when being helped by a
therapist
is different from
being helped by a friend
or loved one

There is quite a lot of concern expressed in the media about the infiltration of counselling and psychotherapy into our personal lives. Some of the imagery that some journalists employ suggest that there is a battle for the psyche going on. Thus, 'armies' of counsellors are portrayed descending on the scene of some tragedy or other, intervening to prevent the masses from developing post-traumatic stress disorder. In other cases, people with more money than sense are pilloried for checking themselves into 'a top private clinic' (usually the Priory Hospital at Roehampton) when they would be far better off, according to the writer, having a few early nights. Thus, people are either portrayed as victims who need protecting from the marauding hordes of counsellors or spoilt brats who counsellors are quite willing to exploit for huge sums of money.

A few years ago, the television consumer programme 'Watchdog' arranged for one of its staff to pose as a 'client' and to consult three counsellors for a 'trivial' problem for which counselling was not indicated. Two of the three counsellors recommended ongoing counselling and the other was equivocal. The conclusion that the programme came to was that counsellors were a bunch of opportunists who were looking to make an easy buck. Instead of consulting such charlatans, people are advised to talk to their friends or loved ones.

Leaving aside the question of whether professionally qualified counsellors and psychotherapists are charlatans, can our friends and loved ones provide better help than highly qualified strangers? This question raises a number of complex issues, which I will attempt to address with specific reference to my work as a cognitive-behaviour therapist.

Let me briefly describe cognitive-behaviour therapy before returning to these complex issues. Cognitive-behaviour therapy (CBT) is a tradition in psychotherapy which has its roots in Epictetus's famous dictum that people are disturbed not by things, but by the views that they take of them. These views (or more commonly, thoughts and beliefs) influence and are sustained by the way we behave in the world. In understanding the way that you feel, therefore, cognitive-behaviour therapists are primarily interested in the way that you think and in the way that you act. In helping you over your emotional problems, CBT therapists will help you (a) to identify, question and change salient thoughts and beliefs that are manifestly inconsistent with reality, illogical and dysfunctional; and (b) to act in ways that will strengthen an alternative set of thoughts and beliefs that are consistent with reality, logical and functional. Not content with helping you to do this, CBT therapists will help you to do this for yourself so that you can become your own therapist, as it were.

Now your friends and loved ones may well help you in similar ways and sometimes this will be very helpful. You may become so locked into one way of viewing things that you cannot see the wood from the trees because you are emotionally invested in the subject at hand. A well-meaning friend or loved one may listen to you empathically and because they are not so invested in the issue may point out some things that help you to put the matter into a more objective perspective. We have all probably had the experience of saying to a friend or loved one who has helped us in this way: 'Of course! Why didn't I think of that?' When this happens, it is usually with issues that are acute in nature rather than chronic. With more chronic issues, your friends and loved ones may be at a loss once their opening helping gambits have failed to encourage you to see things from a different perspective.

Let me give an example of this latter issue from my clinical practice. I once saw a woman who was racked with guilt over an abortion she had several years earlier. The circumstances were as follows. She became pregnant after a one-night stand and there were several factors. First, she was a staunch Catholic; second, an early scan showed that the child had spina bifida; and third, she was told that if she had the baby, she could risk her life. After much internal struggle and counselling on this issue she decided to have an abortion. However, she was convinced that she was a bad person who had murdered another human being and as a result would rot in hell.

When I saw her, all of her family members, friends and relatives had pointed out to her repeatedly that she had nothing to blame herself for in deciding to have an abortion. After all, they reasoned, what other option did she have? If she had the child there was a good chance that she would die and who would then look after the child? What kind of life would a child with spina bifida have without a caring mother to look after him or her? Virtually every one of her female friends and relatives assured her that faced with this situation they would have opted for the termination. My client's response to these attempts to help was always to feel reassured for a brief period of time and then to return to being racked with guilt.

When I saw her, I took a different tack and one which shows clearly the difference between a lay and a professional response. What did I do that was different and why was it more successful? Instead of encouraging her to focus on the seemingly good reasons for the abortion, I asked her to assume temporarily that she was right and that she had killed another human being. I helped her to see that her extreme feelings of guilt derived not from this 'fact' but from her attitude towards herself for committing this 'crime'. I showed her that underpinning her guilt were two related beliefs. First, she was demanding that she absolutely should not have killed another human being. Second, she viewed herself as an evil person for doing what she absolutely should not have done. Moreover, I helped her to see that the healthy alternative to her feelings of guilt about killing her unborn child was feelings of remorse. In order to feel remorseful, rather than guilty about what she had done, I helped my client to challenge and change her demanding and self-condemning beliefs and helped her to think as follows: 'I would have much preferred not to have killed my unborn child, but tragically there is no law of the universe decreeing that I absolutely should not have done so. If there was, then it would have been impossible for me to have had the abortion. I am not an evil person for having the abortion. Rather, I am a fallible human being who, again tragically, did a very bad thing'.

Once I had helped my client to develop these healthy beliefs about having the abortion and once she had begun to gain real conviction in them a very interesting thing happened. She spontaneously began to take into account the mitigating factors that she could not consider for long when she was consumed with guilt about having the abortion. Accepting herself for her 'crime' freed her to realise that as a human being she took a course of action that was the lesser of two evils. Once she had given up the demand that she absolutely should have sacrificed herself for her unborn child and once she realised that she certainly would not have advised any of her close friends to have done the same, she appreciated that human being are often faced with very difficult dilemmas which have tragic outcomes no matter which course of action one chooses. Her developing self-acceptance also helped her to see that choosing one's own life over the life of an unborn child is not a despicably selfish act as she had previously thought, but one which reflected a healthy philosophy of enlightened self-interest where one puts one's interests first and those of others a close second.

Herein lies the major difference between a professional response and a lay response. A lay response in this case was to try to convince the person in effect that she hadn't murdered her unborn child and that she had no real choice but to have the abortion. The lay response focuses on the logic of the situation. A professional response, by contrast, focuses on the 'psycho-logic' of the situation. It doesn't set out initially to convince the client that she hadn't murdered her child and that she had no choice but to have the abortion. Rather, it is based on a professional understanding of the dynamics of guilt: that people feel guilty about their perceived wrongdoings not because of the wrongdoings but by their beliefs about their wrongdoings and that once a person holds a demanding and self-condemning set of beliefs about a wrongdoing you have very little chance of encouraging them to take an objective and compassionate view of why they did what they did. It follows from this that the best way of encouraging someone to address their guilt constructively is to first have them assume temporarily that they have committed a wrongdoing and then to understand that their feelings of guilt stems from the demanding and self-condemning beliefs that they hold about the wrongdoing. Helping someone to challenge and change these beliefs helps them to take that objective and compassionate view of their behaviour which the lay response attempts to engender. The professional response argues that the lay response is bound to fail in the long term because it does not address the psychological aspects of the situation. Indeed, the lay response is bound to fail because it does not even appreciate the existence of these psychological aspects.

Let me sum up my position so far. I am arguing that in situations where a person does not have chronic problem based on the existence of long-standing rigid beliefs a lay response may be effective, particularly where that response takes into account the psychological aspects of the situation. But in situations where a person does have a chronic problem based on rigid beliefs and where complicated psychological factors are at work then a lay response is almost bound to be ineffective, particularly because it does not understand and therefore cannot address the complex psychological factors that are at work in the situation.

I frequently observe the lay response at work in the therapy groups that I run based on cognitive-behaviour therapy principles and that take place in the setting of a psychiatric hospital. The patients that are on the CBT programme that I am involved with are taught how to assess and intervene with their own problems. They are taught to use the same skills with themselves that therapists are taught to use with their own patients. In teaching the patients how to be their own therapists, it could be said that we are training them to respond professionally with themselves and with other patients on the programme. But here is the rub. When they are in group therapy and talk directly to one another, they tend not to respond at the professional level that I have been discussing. Thus, they tend not to inquire about the beliefs that underpin their respective disturbances. Rather they tend to give one another practical, common-sense advice which might be useful after they have dealt with their underlying unhealthy beliefs, but is generally ineffective if these latter beliefs are left intact. This lay response continues even when patients are encouraged to respond at the professional level.

It is perhaps unsurprising that lay people should act like lay people even in a therapy group. My point here is to stress that when lay people make a lay response to someone who has a complex and long-standing psychological problem then such a response has distinct limits. It also has limits with less chronic and complex problems when the response ignores the 'psycho-logical' aspects of the problem and concentrates on the logical aspects of the situation. A lay response is effective, then, when the person being helped can respond productively to the logic being offered by the lay helper. When the person being helped cannot do so then the lay helper tends to run out of ideas and tends to repeat the logical response first offered. An impasse soon ensues. At this point, the lay helper should suggest that the person seek a professional response to their problems.

One area where a lay response is often helpful concerns the offering of an empathic response to another's concerns. When you confide in a friend or loved one and they appear to understand your experience and perhaps even link this to a similar experience of their own while recognising the uniqueness of your own experience, this can be liberating for the discloser. Such a response often serves several purposes at the same time. Apart from the therapeutic value of being understood, there is the recognition that one is being accepted for having the experience and not condemned as one fears one might be. If the empathy is combined with self-disclosure of a similar experience on the part of the listener, the discloser has a sense of connectedness with the rest of humanity. 'I'm not the only person who has experienced this' is a common refrain here. This therapeutic factor is called 'universality' in the professional psychotherapy literature. However, there are instances where the lay person is unable to provide an empathic response to the other where a professional is more capable of doing so. The first of these circumstances relates to out of the ordinary, difficult-to-understand experiences. One of my clients confided in a friend that she hoped that her sister would lose her unborn baby. This was too much for the friend to hear and she quickly made her apologies and left, leaving my client crushed and ashamed. A professional would have recognised the dynamics of unhealthy envy at play and would have been able to help the person to see that she wished her sister to miscarry because she resented the fact that her sister with whom she had always had a rivalrous relationship was pregnant when she was experiencing great difficulty getting pregnant herself. One of the capacities that a professional therapist should ideally have is the ability to hear things that lay persons would find shocking without experiencing shock oneself. Of course, therapists are human beings first and foremost and each of us have our limits in this respect, but I would say that this is a significant area where professionally trained psychotherapists have an advantage over lay people in the helping stakes.

Another area in which therapists have an advantage over friends and loved ones occurs when we consider the dangers of being overinvolved as a helper. Since therapists are not involved in their client's life they can take a far more dispassionate stance towards the person's problems where friends and loved ones, given their investment in the person's life, may be too involved to stand back and be dispassionate. Also, it is a skill to be at once dispassionate and empathic and this dual response is one that needs cultivating over time in training and supervision. Some lay persons can do this spontaneously, but most are not able to do so, particularly if they are significantly involved in what the other person is telling them.

Finally, it is difficult for a friend or loved one to offer someone a therapeutic response if the person's problems relate to oneself. One of my clients recently broke up with her lover who kept ringing her to talk about his feelings about the break-up. As one might expect, my client found this enormously difficult to respond to. As she said to me: 'He wants me to be his therapist while at the same time to be able to express his bitterness to me about the way we ended'. As I often say to people, 'if you are emotionally involved with someone you are probably the last person to be able to help them if their problems are about you'.

Lay people help one another with their emotional problems all the time and long may this continue. To reside all therapeutic responses in the consulting rooms of professional counsellors and therapists would be both dangerous and impossible to achieve and this is not what the profession wants to see either. What I have endeavoured to do in this chapter is to show when a professional response is called for and why it is likely to be more therapeutic than the help offered by lay persons, particularly when the latter are socially or intimately involved in the lives of the person needing help. There is a place for professional therapy. Let's not exaggerate this place, but let's not minimise it either.

8

the name change debate: Ellis's real agenda

In this brief outline, I reveal for the first time Albert Ellis's real agenda for recently changing the name from Rational-Emotive Therapy (RET) to Rational Emotive Behaviour Therapy (REBT). As is now well known, in 1993 Albert Ellis (1995) changed the name of the therapy that he originally devised from Rational-Emotive Therapy (RET) to Rational Emotive Behaviour Therapy (REBT). In an issue of the *Journal of Rational-Emotive and Cognitive-Behavior Therapy,* Davison (1995) is supportive of this name change, while Franks (1995) and Lazarus (1995) voice their doubts about this new development. Unfortunately, both Davison and Franks fail to discern Ellis's true purpose in changing the name and while Lazarus is on the right track in speculating that REBT is only a forerunner to future name changes, he also fails to determine Ellis's real intention. Ellis, in his article, understandably chooses not to 'come clean'. By closely analysing the content and timing of the name changes that have been made so far, I can reveal for the first time that the next, and penultimate, name change will occur in 1999 and the final change will occur in the year 2031. Here is my reasoning.

Rational therapy was originally devised in 1955 and gained the acronym RT. Note closely that RT are two letters from the name 'Albert'. So we have:

1955 = RT

Six years later, Ellis decided to change the name of Rational Therapy to Rational-Emotive Therapy to reflect the fact that the therapy did not neglect emotions. Thus, RT became RET. Note closely that the addition of the 'E' is yet another letter from the name 'Albert'. Thus we now have:

1961 = RET

Thirty two years on, Ellis decides on another name change. He argues (Ellis, 1995) that he was wrong not to include RET's decided behavioural emphasis in the name of his therapy; so in 1993 RET became REBT. Note that the inclusion of the new letter 'B' is yet another letter from the name 'Albert'. We now have:

1993 = REBT

My first hypothesis, based on an examination of the data presented so far, is that in 1999 (i.e. six years from 1993 — remember that the first name change came at the end of a six-year cycle), Ellis will make a fourth change and introduce yet another letter from his name. Recently, Ellis (1991) has claimed that critics have not appreciated that RET/REBT is not only concerned with helping people to overcome their psychological problems, it is also concerned with helping people to ACTUALISE themselves. So my first hypothesis states that in 1999, Ellis will change the name of the therapy to 'Actualising Rational Emotive Behaviour Therapy' or AREBT. Note that subtle introduction of the 'A' — yet another letter from the name 'Albert'. So:

1999 = AREBT

If my first hypothesis is supported then I can confidently present my second hypothesis which is that: Thirty-two years after the fourth name change, a fifth and final name change will occur (remember that RET became REBT after a gap of 32 years). Ellis has often noted that RET/REBT advocates the use of humour in that it helps people to laugh at their silly ideas (e.g. Ellis, 1987). Humour, then helps people to take themselves seriously, but not too seriously — an important ingredient of psychological health. The use of humour also qualifies as a neglected aspect of REBT. Now, I do admit that there is a problem with this analysis in that the 'H' from humour does not appear in the name 'Albert'. Then it occurred to me. Humour, per se, is not the curative factor here — LAUGHTER is. And 'L' is the missing letter from the name 'Albert'. So finally we have:

2031 = ALBERT

And what does 'ALBERT' stand for? It stands for:

ACTUALISING LAUGHTER-BASED BEHAVIOURAL EMOTIVE RATIONAL THERAPY

The fact that Albert Ellis will be 118 years old when he makes this final change is, I admit, problematic. But since he has often claimed that Duracell will some day invent a battery that one can insert up one's behind enabling one to live forever, who knows!

In my next paper, I will reveal the shocking truth about what happened to the hyphen when Rational-Emotive Therapy became Rational Emotive Behaviour Therapy.

References

Davison, G. C. (1995). Personal reflections on Albert Ellis and rational emotive behavior therapy. *Journal of Rational-Emotive and Cognitive-Behavior Therapy, 13,* 81–4.

Ellis, A. (1987). The use of rational humorous songs in psychotherapy. In W. F. Fry Jr. & W. A. Salameh (eds.), *Handbook of Humor in Psychotherapy: Advances in the Clinical use of Humor.* Sarasota, FL: Professional Resource Exchange Inc.

Ellis, A. (1991). Achieving self-actualization. In A. Jones & R. Crandall (eds.), *Handbook of Self-actualization.* Corte Madera, CA: Select Press.

Ellis, A. (1995). Changing rational-emotive therapy (RET) to rational emotive behavior therapy (REBT). *Journal of Rational-Emotive and Cognitive-Behavior Therapy, 13,* 85–9.

Franks, C. M. (1995). RET, REBT, and Albert Ellis. *Journal of Rational-Emotive and Cognitive-Behavior Therapy, 13,* 91–5.

Lazarus, A. A. (1995). REBT: A sign of evolution or devolution? An historical perspective. *Journal of Rational-Emotive and Cognitive-Behavior Therapy, 13,* 97–100.

9

Albert Ellis:
man of letters

In this chapter, I reveal that Albert Ellis does actualise his gene for efficiency in the practice of REBT. This is shown in his decreasing use of words and in a corresponding increase in the use of letters and acronyms. A transcript of one of Ellis's therapy sessions is used to demonstrate this in action.

Albert Ellis has often said in workshops that he has a gene for efficiency. This is reflected in his writings on the theory and practice of REBT where there is an increasing use of letters and of acronyms instead of words. Thus, rather than refer to low frustration tolerance, Ellis (and other REBT therapists) use the acronym LFT. Recent additions to this growing list of acronyms is 'USA' (unconditional self-acceptance) and 'PYA' (push your ass). But is Ellis using such acronyms in his therapeutic practice? The following transcript of Ellis conducting therapy with an anxious client provides an affirmative answer.

Albert: What is your first name?

Dee: My first name is Dee.

Albert: OK, Dee, what problem would you like to start with?

Dee: Well, Dr Ellis, I have quite an unusual problem. I really love sailing on the sea, but every time I go I become afraid that I might see a swarm of bees and when I get afraid I shout out 'Ay!'

Ellis: OK, Dee. In REBT we use an ABC model where A is the event and C is your emotional and behavioural response to that event. Now in your case, A is the bees at sea and C is 'Ay'. But, in REBT we say that A doesn't cause C. So, the bees at sea don't cause 'Ay!' Rather it is B, your belief system, that largely determines C. So, what are you telling yourself at B to make yourself shout out 'Ay!' at C when you see the bees at sea at A, Dee?

Dee: . . . I'm not sure, Dr Ellis . . .

Albert: Well, you're not telling yourself: 'I hope I see bees at sea,' are you?

Dee: Oh, I see. No, I'm not telling myself that. I'm telling myself 'I couldn't bear it if I saw the bees at sea'.

Albert: That's exactly right. You have LFT at B, about the bees at sea at A that makes you shout out 'Ay!' at C, Dee.

Dee: So, how do I get over my problem, Dr Ellis?

Albert: By developing a philosophy of HFT about the bees at sea at A, so you get a healthier response at C, Dee. This new C is your G or goal.

Dee: What would be my G?

Albert: Concern about the prospect of seeing the bees at sea or disappointment about actually seeing them.

Dee: Actually when I'm concerned, I shout out 'Eeee!'

Albert: Alright. So what you have to do in order to shout out 'Eeee!' at C rather than 'Ay!' at C about the bees at sea at A, Dee, is to dispute your LFT until you develop HFT.

Dee: That sounds clear, but how do I do this?

Albert: By going to D, Dee.

Dee: DD?

Albert: No, not DD — D, Dee where D stands for disputing.

Dee: Oh!

Albert: So where is the evidence that you can't stand to see the bees at sea at A?

Dee: My feelings tell me that I can't.

Albert (sarcastically): 'Oh, my feelings, my feelings'. Horseshit! Your sacred feelings at C stem from your B about the bees at sea at A and prove that you have LFT rather than that you truly can't stand seeing the bees at sea at A, Dee.

Dee: But it's too hard for me to dispute my LFT at B about the bees at sea at A.

Albert: Bullshit. That just proves that you are a difficult customer, a DC, Dee, who has LFT about changing her LFT.

Dee: So what do I do about that?

Albert: You push your ass or PYA and force yourself to tolerate your discomfort anxiety or DA while challenging your LFT at B about the bees at sea at A that make you shout out 'Ay!' at C and you keep doing this until you develop HFT at B about seeing the bees at sea at A and achieve your G which is shouting out 'Eeee!' at C instead. Do you see, Dee?

Dee: I see, Dr. Ellis, but I'm scared to do this in case I fail.

Albert: That just proves that you have ego anxiety or EA, Dee.

Dee: So how do I overcome this?

Albert: By developing a philosophy of unconditional self-acceptance or USA about failing to overcome your LFT at B about seeing the bees at sea at A that leads you to shout out 'Ay!' at C, Dee. Showing yourself that you are a fallible human being or FHB for failing will help you to develop USA.

Dee: Are there any techniques to help me with this?

Albert: Yes, rational-emotive imagery or REI. Now, close your eyes and vividly imagine that you are failing to overcome your LFT about seeing the bees at sea at A and make yourself feel depressed at C, Dee. Tell me when you have done that.

Dee: OK.

Albert: Now, while still vividly imagining that you are failing to overcome your LFT about seeing the bees at sea at A, change your feelings from d-pression to disappointment and tell me when you have done that.

Dee: (long pause) . . . OK.

Dee: But it's too hard for me to dispute my LFT at B about the bees at sea at A.

Albert: Bullshit. That just proves that you are a difficult customer, a DC. Dee, who has LFT about changing her LFT.

Dee: So what do I do about that?

Albert: You push your ass or PYA and force yourself to tolerate your discomfort anxiety or DA while challenging your LFT at B about the bees at sea at A that make you shout out 'Ay!' at C and you keep doing this until you develop HFT at B about seeing the bees at sea at A and achieve your G which is shouting out 'Eeee!' at C instead. Do you see, Dee?

Dee: I see, Dr Ellis, but I'm scared to do this in case I fail.

Albert: That just proves that you have ego anxiety or EA, Dee.

Dee: So how do I overcome this?

Albert: By developing a philosophy of unconditional self-acceptance or USA about failing to overcome your LFT at B about seeing the bees at sea at A that leads you to shout out 'Ay!' at C, Dee. Showing yourself that you are a fallible human being or FHB for failing will help you to develop USA.

Dee: Are there any techniques to help me with this?

Albert: Yes, rational-emotive imagery or REI. Now, close your eyes and vividly imagine that you are failing to overcome your LFT about seeing the bees at sea at A and make yourself feel depressed at C, Dee. Tell me when you have done that.

Dee: (long pause) . . . OK.

Albert: How did you do that?

Dee: I told myself that I am an FHB for failing to overcome my LFT about seeing the bees at sea.

Albert: Now practise REL for ten minutes a day for 30 days to develop USA about failing to develop HFT and then use it to develop HFT about seeing the bees at sea at A, Dee. OK?

Dee: OK. But that's a lot to take in, Dr Ellis.

Albert: Let me summarise. When you see the bees at sea at A, Dee, you shout out 'Ay!' at C because you have LFT at B. First, go to D and develop HFT at B about the bees at sea at A until you achieve your G or new C which is shouting out 'Eeee!' As you do this you also need to overcome your DA about addressing your LFT. Don't be a DC and PYA. Then, work to develop USA and show yourself that you are an FHB if you fail to overcome your LFT about seeing the bees at sea at A. Then use REI, first to develop USA at B about your ongoing LFT at A, and then to develop HFT at B about seeing the bees at sea at A. OK?

Dee: A-OK, Dr E.

10

the politically incorrect Professor: Dave Mearns interviews Windy Dryden

Preamble
When they were young, both my daughters took an instant liking to Windy Dryden. Not many adults achieve that immediate 'contact' with young people whose appraisal can be the most searching of all. Windy Dryden became Britain's first Professor of Counselling and has been prolific in his publishing, to date, of 115 books. In the course of that astounding output, Dryden has encouraged and developed scores of other counselling authors. I would not hesitate to argue in support of the motion that Windy Dryden has done more to advance the profession of counselling in Britain than any other person. Yet, in the eyes of many within the profession, he is an enigma. Although a leader in counselling he is frequently not really accepted as 'representative' of the profession. Numerous interviews have been done with Windy Dryden — he has even published a book of them! (Dryden & Vasco, 1991). In this interview I wanted to try to get at this apparent paradox between Windy Dryden's contribution and his persona within the profession. Who is this man with whom so many in the profession feel 'uncomfortable'? What is the nature of his 'differentness'? Does the general impression of him tell us more about our profession than about him? After all, were my daughters more accurate in their impression of Windy Dryden as a warm, friendly man who was easy to relate to?

The following interview was recorded on Sunday, 16 May, 1999. The transcript has been tidied rather than edited.

The interview
Dave: Windy, sometimes when I mention your name to others in the counselling world they raise their eyes. Then, when I say that I'm a friend of yours, they say, 'Are you?' with considerable incredulity in their voice. What do you think this is about, Windy?

Windy: I don't know. I don't really mix that much in counselling circles any more, partly because I don't enjoy hanging around with lots of counsellors en masse. I would rather watch Tottenham Hotspur than actually go to a BAC conference.

Dave: That must be really bad, Windy, if you'd rather watch Tottenham Hotspur because I know you're an ardent Arsenal fan! How do you think you are seen?

Windy: I don't know, but I could hazard a guess.

Dave: What would that guess be?

Windy: I imagine that I'm seen as an abrupt type who is sort of in the mould of Albert Ellis.

Dave: So, you might be classed with him because you practise the same approach to therapy?

Windy: That could well be the case. However, as I don't hang out that much with counsellors it's difficult for me to know exactly what they think of me. *(pause)* Some people think I'm a woman.

Dave: Of course, 'Wendy'!

Windy: I once had a conversation with somebody in a bookshop. She was holding one of my books and I just said to her: 'Oh yes it's Windy Dryden, he publishes a lot, doesn't he?', so she said to me — 'oh no, she's a woman' — Politely, I added, 'I don't think she is you know' — only to be defeated with, 'Well I've actually seen her lecture'.

Dave: Oh my God!

Windy: I also don't tend to keep in touch with a lot of my ex-students so I don't have a large coterie of followers. Also, I don't have too many friends in the counselling world because I prefer to have a personal life *outside* of that world.

Dave: And do you believe you are, in a way, not very much like most counsellors?

Windy: I would say *yes*, but it's hard for me to tell really because there is a difference between the public persona and the private self of many counsellors. In my view there is not too much of a discrepancy between my public persona and my private self. I can be brusque in my private life and I can also be brusque publicly. I don't have what may be called a public therapeutic 'manner' where I ooze warmth and understanding and no doubt that has permeated the consciousness of the counselling world.

Dave: Would you say that you're not very politically correct?

Windy: That's true. Recently, I received a verbal warning at Goldsmiths

College because sometimes I curse in class. Actually, I believe that counselling students need to be comfortable with profanity and I sometimes use profanity in a training setting but never at my students, but certainly *with* them. Anyway, one of my students anonymously complained and the College acted on it, which was strange as it was anonymous. I still hold that it is not the crime of the century but the College deemed otherwise — so that's a very good example of political 'incorrectness'. I do firmly believe that counselling has to be careful in its alignment with political correctness. I believe firmly that counsellors need to create an environment which allows clients to be politically *incorrect*.

Dave: You mean that's what they *should* do.

Windy: I think so.

Dave: Yeah — that it actually should be creating a context which allows clients to behave in a broader range of ways.

Windy: Right, I recently told of my experience at College to someone that I know and he said that he would actually discourage his clients from swearing because he finds that language offensive. I just could not believe that.

Dave: Astonishing.

Windy: It would be interesting to have an open debate about this issue and what annoyed me at College was that this didn't happen. What should have been forum for debate was a forum for censure.

Dave: Gosh, that must have been really sore — I would have felt really sore, particularly with all that happening anonymously.

Windy: Interestingly enough all the students in that year, including presumably the person who complained about me, actually wrote a letter to College saying that they did not find my language offensive at all. In fact when I told my current group of students the story they said that they would write a letter of complaint about me if I *didn't* swear! Yes, it wasn't an easy time, but I was very naïve in trusting certain people in College who offered a supportive hand and then twisted it and used it against me.

Dave: Let you 'swing' — goodness gracious. That's frightening, because I mean I would have to, for instance, do away with my 'Billy Connolly' routine which is a major part of my lecturing when I'm trying to get people to use their imagination and their perceptiveness — it's really crazy. It's different swearing at someone but just using words, that's different.

Windy: Yes, I certainly don't hold with swearing at students. The other thing which I'm politically incorrect about concerns punctuality. I hold very dear the importance of punctuality in training students and I have been known to lock out students who have a terminal lateness problem. I don't do it immediately, of course. I do talk to them about it up to three times, but then when I see that they are not listening to my words, I get them to learn by action. I am sure that other tutors don't lock out their students because I'm sure that on most courses students turn up on time. Although I do recall going up to Scotland once to work on a certain person-centred course and a sizeable minority of students didn't turn up.

Dave: I know, I know, I know Windy — it was my course. I spoke with them about it.

Windy: I would have flogged them!

Dave: (Laughter)

Windy: So you see I'm hardly a model of political correctness with all this swearing and locking students going on.

Dave: I like students being punctual too — so I customarily say at the beginning of a course, 'look I'll start the lectures on time — even if you are not here I'll start on time'. One course absolutely got me the next week — *none* of them were there on time! One of them popped their head round the door and said, 'Have you started yet?'

Windy: Right, yeah. That's happened to me and I <u>did</u> start!

Dave: (Laughter)

Windy: I am sure that this kind of behaviour, which is unusual for a counselling trainer — although it doesn't happen very often —

does travel along the counselling wire and leaves people making inferences about me rather than seeing the whole person. I think that counsellors find it very difficult to see the whole person of other counsellors.

Dave: You're aware of your controversiality yourself — like in your book of public lectures, *Are you Sitting Uncomfortably? Windy Dryden Live and Uncut* (Dryden, 1998). I mean, one of your lectures is the famous, or infamous, 'Dublin' lecture where someone actually walked out very publicly. What was that all about?

Windy: I have no idea. I mean I actually gave a talk which was entitled 'The Counsellor as Educator' and in that talk I discussed the idea that one role, not the only role, that a counsellor can adopt is one where we educate people psychologically. This apparently offended some people — although again you see — one of the things about the counselling world I'm afraid is that very few people will come up to me and say, 'we heard your lecture and we fundamentally disagree with it.' I mean I heard on the grapevine that there were a number of people even arguing that I should not be awarded a Fellowship from the British Association for Counselling because of it. Now it would be nice if people had the guts to come up and talk to me directly or even to write so I can respond. But, that doesn't happen.

Dave: I was at that lecture and perhaps the most controversial thing that I remember was that, at a counselling conference, you were actually saying counselling hadn't helped *you* — what had been helpful, and might be helpful for others, was a good self-help book.

Windy: Yes, and I think that may be seen as a threat — although God knows why, because I'm only talking about my experience. I am not suggesting that we actually replace counsellors with good books, although I'm sure that several of my good books are more effective than some counsellors!

Dave: (Laughter)

Windy: It's that kind of remark that gets me into trouble, you see!

Dave: Yes.

Windy: I suppose you won't edit that bit out.

Dave: That's right. But, isn't there something enigmatic about it — I mean 115 books on counselling and yet you have nothing good to say about your own experience of being a client. Four times you've been a client and you've nothing good to say about any of them?

Windy: No, I wouldn't say 'nothing'. I mean, the second one was with somebody who was loosely psychodynamic but also used psychodrama methods and those were quite useful, the more active methods. The fourth was with a Jungian therapist who I got on with but we got a bit bogged down because I couldn't remember any of my dreams. I don't have the psychological makeup to benefit from psychoanalytical therapy, I really don't — I'm not saying therefore that all psychodynamic therapies are crap because that's obviously not true.

Dave: It's just that the 'fit' wasn't right for you. What does work for you — I have been picking this up from reading is, in a sense, being your *own* therapist. It's like you can give yourself the conditions that are right for you, in terms of your own . . . I was going to say 'meditation' — but that's a misleading word — more your 'contemplation' . . .

Windy: But then the old joke is — the only trouble with self-therapy is with the countertransference! Yes, I mean I was helped more by reading one of Albert Ellis's books than I was with the therapists that I actually consulted.

Dave: In reading your book of lectures, the one I enjoyed most must also have been incredibly controversial. It was the 1997 lecture to the first International Conference on Counselling Psychology. I mean, you preface the lecture by saying you think that it is probably your most controversial and yet I have also talked with someone who was there and they said there wasn't a murmur, in the sense that there wasn't a dissenting murmur.

Windy: Well I kind of set it up, after the Dublin experience. In Dublin, if I had gone in there and said, 'I'm sure that loads of people are going to be offended by this', then I think everybody would have said, 'oh no I'm far too tolerant and mature to be offended by this!'

Dave: So you pre-empted it?

Windy: I kind of pre-empted it, yes. Not as a deliberate ploy because I really did think that despite this particular 'warning', people would still have been offended.

Dave: One of the things, for instance, you said in that lecture was that women are disturbed not by being raped but by their rigid and extreme views of being raped. I know what you are about there, in terms of Rational Emotive Behaviour Therapy, and you took great care over the presentation, but that is just so against the grain, or against the counselling culture, you knew that you should expect huge reactions.

Windy: Yeah, but you see what I make clear in that lecture is that I didn't then, and do not now, condone rape which I regard as something extraordinarily negative. And that it is healthy for women, in this case, to be, if you like, 'healthily' distressed — *very* distressed about this. However, my point is that some of the conclusions that women make about being raped are not intrinsic parts of that experience and that was the thing I was actually talking about. If it was an intrinsic part of the experience then I would obviously argue that they could not be held responsible for these conclusions. I think that when we talk about 'responsibility' in that area, people often immediately think about 'blame' and, as if I'm blaming rape victims for their own traumatised reaction, which of course I'm not doing. So, I mean, if people were to read the arguments clearly, there would be no difficulty.

Dave: In a sense, if people can read or listen to the argument then it can make sense, but if you only get second hand 'sound bites', then it gets mixed up with people's own irrational thinking in a way.

Windy: That's right.

Dave: I was thinking about this 'enigmatic' quality of Windy Dryden. I wonder if one of the difficulties about you is that you are 'normal', in the sense that you boldly, obstinately refuse to be 'neurotic'. And the norm in our profession *must* be in the direction of neurosis.

Windy: Well that's right, that's why I'm very much ambivalent about the personal therapy requirement. People who attend my courses say, 'oh, do we have to be in personal therapy?', and my response is 'only if you need it'.

Obviously, I have my vulnerabilities just like anybody else, but I think that I am a reasonably well-adjusted individual in a number of areas.

Dave: And of course 'normality' would be potentially frightening if the norm within the counselling world is 'neurotic'.

Windy: It could very well be.

Dave: You were talking about yourself there, Windy, and I had one or two questions on that. One of the questions is quite simple — are you a 'loner'?

Windy: I wouldn't say that I'm a loner, but I definitely enjoy my own company and I have the ability to be alone and pursue my own personal projects for fairly long periods of time. So yes, in that sense — I'm a loner. Being an only child was a help for that.

Dave: I have always felt that that was fundamental for me too.

Windy: Yeah, but I can also mix with people. Not, as I say, with counsellors that much, particularly en masse — I find them quite a frustrating experience. But certainly going to the Arsenal with my friends and 'laddish' things like around the Leisure Centre where I'm a member, I find interaction with others very enjoyable.

Dave: What 'unhealthy negative emotions' are you prone to, Windy? I mean 'depression', 'guilt', 'anxiety'. Let me guess, 'depression' more than the other two?

Windy: No, you're wrong.

Dave: Interesting.

Windy: I very rarely, if ever, get depressed these days. I was moderately depressed in my early twenties for which I did seek therapy, which as I have said was not very helpful. No, I think of all the unhealthy negative emotions I'm most prone to unhealthy anger.

I think I've inherited, from the male side of my family, a tendency to easily make myself 'unhealthily' angry. On top of that I still do feel 'healthily' angry at times. I think people find it hard to notice the difference and at times it may spill over, from 'healthy' to 'unhealthy', but I'm quite prone to anger in both its forms.

Dave: Yeah, and I can see in that situation that it would be difficult for the other person to know the difference between 'healthy' and 'unhealthy' anger. But 'anger' is your vulnerability more than the others?

Windy: Definitely.

Dave: How about 'irrational beliefs', any irrational beliefs that still trip you up?

Windy: Yes, I think one. I have the belief that other people must not try to shortcut things and if they do they must not get away with it. When people do benefit from taking professional shortcuts I find that most difficult to deal with.

For example, a couple of years ago, I was asked to sit on a promotions panel for someone in a field close to our own. I discovered that the person's PhD did not contain any data and I brought this to the attention of the panel at the University. However, they were completely unconcerned about it, which really surprised me. The person eventually was awarded a professorship, which I found difficult to stomach. So it's events like this that I struggle most with.

Dave: Right.

Windy: Anyway eventually I take myself in hand and accept that things like this are going to happen in our world and that there is no inherent justice in the world to prevent it from happening. So I strive to tolerate it while actively disliking it.

Dave: That, in a sense, leads neatly on to my next question: what are you *passionate* about in life, Windy? And, by the way, I have already noted down Arsenal! What are you passionate about in life?

Windy: I'm passionate about helping people to live meaningful lives without needlessly disturbing themselves. That's why I spend a lot of my time writing and I am at the moment increasingly writing 'self-help' books, which, in an academic environment, gets you no credit whatsoever. But writing self-help books is one of my abiding passions. I have quite a few other passions — for example I enjoy the Marx Brothers movies, I go over these when I have some time. I'm also a great fan of Al Jolson and Junior Walker and the All Stars. I like Sergeant Bilko, the Billy Bunter novels of Frank Richards. I am passionate about Gregorian music, and steam trains and . . .

Dave: You realise of course, Windy, they are all still in the 'black and white' era — you haven't reached the 'colour' era.

Windy: I know, and I avidly like boxing. Of course, that is another politically incorrect thing for counsellors to follow.

Dave: Which will worry you a lot!

Windy: Right, now I realise that I'm listing my 'interests' rather than my 'passions', but I tend to be passionate about my interests. But on the whole my greatest passion is to help people become healthier in a variety of ways. This is the other thing, *variety* is important to me. I think it will be interesting to see what happens with the Internet in the years to come, if we can help some people through that medium.

Dave: As you were talking, what immediately came to my mind was a person who could take the step of buying a self-help book off a railway stand but, by God, would be a hundred miles away from actually seeking contact with another human being for help.

Windy: That's right.

Dave: And the Internet would fit that too, wouldn't it?

Windy: Yeah, that's right.

Dave: Somebody who could make contact through that medium but would find it really difficult to go to counselling. Boy, there must be almost a majority of them — a huge number that counselling never sees.

Windy: That's right. I think that this is where we again get into developing psychological education which, as you know, is one of my passions.

Dave: One of the books I loved in the last year is Firestone's book on suicide (Firestone, 1997). He paints this incredibly vivid picture of the young, often young *male*, who is so cut off from others. And I've often thought, gosh yes, counselling isn't the medium for reaching that person. They would not *engage*.

Dave: Last question, Windy. What *challenges* are there for you in the future? Is it the second century of books?

Windy: Oh no, no, no. I mean I do have writing plans. One of my goals is to have a self-help book for every major emotional disturbance people have. I have brought one out on shame, guilt, anger, jealousy and sulking. I haven't yet touched anxiety and depression, although I'm going to get around to those. That is one particular goal. But all I really want is just to continue doing the things now I enjoy and find meaningful. One of the things I like about my life is its variety. People often assume, wrongly, that I don't see clients and in fact I see a fair number because I believe that it is important to keep one's skills up to scratch for training purposes. I'm just going to take life as it comes and actually kind of enjoy life a lot and let's see what actually happens. I don't have any particular ambitions and goals because I've achieved quite a lot of them already.

Dave: That's it — Windy, thanks very much indeed.

Windy: Bye.

References

Dryden, W. (1998) *Are you sitting uncomfortably? Windy Dryden Live and Uncut.* Ross-on-Wye: PCCS Books.

Dryden, W. & Vasco, A. (1991) *Dryden on Counselling Volume 2: A Dialogue.* London: Whurr.

Firestone, R. (1997) *Suicide and the Inner Voice.* Thousand Oaks, CA: Sage.